Haunted
Richmond, Virginia

Pamela K. Kinney

4880 Lower Valley Road   Atglen, Pennsylvania   19310

Dedication

This book is dedicated to all those interested in the paranormal happenings in our world. It is also dedicated to all those who I interviewed and received much information from, as I tried to bring forth not only the supernatural occurrences that happened at the various places in the book, but also the rich history that is uniquely Richmond's.

I'd like to thank my husband, Bill, for his patience while I researched and wrote this book, and even for his help on some field trips. I'd also like to thank Linda Lyons for her invaluable time in helping me with last minute editing advice; same goes to Peg Stotts, and to Mark Layne for helping this camera-dysfunctional person. Dedication also goes to the writer's groups I frequent, also to my friends and to my son, Chris, who believes in ghosts, too. Last but not least, to Edgar Allan Poe, Richmond's own native son. May his *Tell-Tale Heart* never die; nevermore!

Published by Schiffer Publishing Ltd.
4880 Lower Valley Road
Atglen, PA 19310
Phone: (610) 593-1777; Fax: (610) 593-2002
E-mail: Info@schifferbooks.com

For the largest selection of fine reference books on this and related subjects, please visit our web site at
www.schifferbooks.com
We are always looking for people to write books on new and related subjects. If you have an idea for a book please contact us at the above address.

This book may be purchased from the publisher.
Include $3.95 for shipping.
Please try your bookstore first.
You may write for a free catalog.

In Europe, Schiffer books are distributed by
Bushwood Books
6 Marksbury Ave.
Kew Gardens
Surrey TW9 4JF England
Phone: 44 (0) 20 8392-8585; Fax: 44 (0) 20 8392-9876
E-mail: info@bushwoodbooks.co.uk
Website: www.bushwoodbooks.co.uk
Free postage in the U.K., Europe; air mail at cost.

Copyright © 2007 by Pamela K. Kinney
Library of Congress Control Number: 2007925059

Designed by Mark David Bowyer
Type set in Batik Regular / Souvenir Lt BT

ISBN: 978-0-7643-2712-4
Printed in China

Contents

And thou, a ghost, amid the entombing trees

Didst glide away. Only thine eyes remained;

They would not go—they never yet have gone;

Lighting my lonely pathway home that night,

They have not left me (as my hopes have) since;

They follow me—they lead me through the years.

To Helen by Edgar Allan Poe (1809-1849)

Introduction

When I mentioned I was writing a book on the paranormal activities of Richmond, Virginia, I was asked by people if I really believed in *all that stuff*. I just looked at them and answered, "Yes. Yes, I do."

When I was growing up, experiences of the supernatural kind became passé. For one example, my mother would have dreams that predicted when my Uncle Joey would mail a letter to us about Grandma's death, or that a girlfriend I hadn't seen in six years would call on the phone—all exactly on the dates she said those things would happen.

But that was just a taste of the phenomena I experienced over the years. Mine weren't dreams, but ghostly encounters. One of these happened at the Whaley House in Old Town, California (located in San Diego). A tourist attraction, the Whaley House is also a historical house, belonging these days to the State of California. I was in the ninth grade when I had my first encounter with that house. My Geography class from El Cajon High School went on a field trip to Old Town. My best friend, Debbie Noonan, and I had just had lunch at Taco Bell across the street from the place, and though we couldn't afford to go inside the house and take the tour, we decided to peek through the windows and check it out.

While Debbie peered though the window that looked into the hall between the entrance and the courtroom (yes, this house held the city court back in the late 1800s), I stared through the window that looked into the courtroom itself. My glance caught a tiny lady, dark hair up in a bun, wearing an old-fashioned dress. She crossed the room, heading for the opened doorway that led to the area Debbie had just stared at some minutes earlier. I thought at the time that she seemed to be walking oddly—floating actually—but didn't think anything more of it. Just before she passed through the entryway, I darted over to the window Debbie had just vacated and peered through it. With shock, I noticed that the lady never came through, and I headed back over to the other window I had left seconds before and found that she wasn't in the courtroom either.

Debbie and I talked about it—about how weird it all was—and we entered the house, walking over to a couple of ladies dressed in regular clothing sitting at a desk.

"Where's the tour guide in the costume?" I asked.

Both ladies just stared at me, and one of them answered that the tour guides didn't wear costumes at all. She then asked me to describe the woman I saw, and so I did. She then told me I had seen the ghost of Mrs. Whaley.

We talked a bit more about the ghosts of the house then, something the tour guides appeared to be very used to. I had a ghostly encounter and had never even been inside the house to have it!

The next time something happened to me was years later. I went inside the house and walked up the stairs to the second floor. I stepped onto what was referred to as the step where people always had experiences. Suddenly, it felt like someone was choking me. It lasted about a minute and when my throat was finally set free, I continued up the stairs to the second floor.

Over the years, I have had other encounters, mostly pleasant ones. There were a couple of nasty ones, though. One of them took place at an apartment my husband and I rented in El Cajon, California when our son was two years old. To this day, I don't even know why it began, as in several months of living there nothing had happened. But one evening, while I was reading in our bedroom as Bill, my husband, sat in the living room watching TV, and our baby son was asleep in his crib in his room, I heard someone climb over the fence that separated the backyards of our place and the one next door. The sounds of someone walking continued, then ended by our bedroom window. Thinking it was the man from next door, I was upset that he was looking in through our window while I lay in bed, especially since the curtains were parted. I turned to look at the window, ready to call Bill about it. No one was there!

For the next year, things kept happening, from the odor of cigarettes in front of our couch (as if someone were smoking) to noises and finding nothing wrong or no one there, to even one night when I woke up to see a man with a nasty look on his face standing there, staring at me. Frightened by actually seeing the ghost, I hid under the covers and never did tell my unsuspecting, sleeping husband.

Bill worked nights, and when he did, I would always grab my son and we would go over to my friend Kathy's apartment until he came home, or when I finally dared to, went back home on my own, so Chris could sleep in his own crib. Eventually, we moved away and I don't know if the ghost remained there or vanished when we went.

We also had another ghost that haunted that apartment. To begin with, we had to put our cat to sleep. One week later, as my friend, Kathy, drove down the street, she noticed the cat lying in the kitchen window. She asked me later over the phone if we had decided not to put him to sleep. I replied that he had been dead for a week. That freaked her out.

And sometimes, something like a small body would leap up onto the mattress of my bed and walk around me, just like he used to.

These weren't the last encounters I had, either! The latest happened when my husband and I walked around Shockoe Bottom to take pictures of various places I had heard were haunted, and one of the places, Castle Thunder Prison, actually gave me something strange on my photos. It was a window that appeared to have a weird flickering light effect when you looked through the viewfinder and yet, looked like a perfectly normal window when I looked with my own eyes. After the picture was taken, my husband and I saw that window had the strange effect of blinds or a shutter covering the window. (You'll be able to see the picture, as this one is included in the Shockoe Bottom chapter. And *no*, I didn't alter any of the photos that are in this book.)

So yes, I do believe in ghosts. Having my own encounters has always made me interested in hearing others, and I try to determine which ones are factual and which ones are made up, or which ones are legends that grew up around a grain of truth. But even legends and myths can be interesting, adding flavor to a house, town, or a person.

I once read that Virginia has been dubbed the most haunted state in the nation. Richmond, and its surrounding counties, and the Tri-Cities, including Petersburg, has certainly added to that surplus of ghostly happenings. With a city that can name Edgar Allan Poe as its native son, and with such a deep 'Old South' flavor, I feel that more than anywhere else in Virginia, Richmond is rich in ghostly lore and tales.

I hope this book will give you, the reader, an inkling of the ghost stories and legends that abound in Richmond. I think, when reading them, you'll also learn something about Richmond: its history, its culture, its way of life. And, besides ghosts, you'll discover that many of the haunted places are interesting museums in their own right, that the restaurants have great food, and that you can take a ghost tour with Haunts of Richmond, which also performs the local ghost stories in a "haunted house" production most of the year.

From the Native American tribes that once inhabited this area, to the white colonists who settled here, to the War for America's Independence—and even the War Between the States—right up until the present day, Richmond has spirits that cause ghostly "bumps in the night."

Whether you believe any of the stories that will be told in the coming chapters is neither here nor there. Read them and decide for yourself, or just enjoy them; but keep the lights on when you do. If you want to really know Richmond, then getting to know its ghosts is another way to understand what makes the city and its surrounding areas tick.

So curl up in a comfortable chair with a cup of tea or coffee nearby, and enjoy unfurling the following pages. Get to know some of Richmond's residents that hang around—even after death.

Haunts of Richmond

Haunts of Richmond is an attraction that opened on 11 N. 18th Street in Shockoe Bottom a couple years ago. On their website, http://www.hauntsofrichmond.com, they claim to bring ghost stories and legends to life. They hold walking ghost tours and a haunted house with themed theatrical productions, mainly on Thursdays, Fridays, and Saturdays most of the year. They are closed during February and March; except they will open by appointment for groups wanting a ghost tour. Gargoyle statues stare out onto the street in the windows, and the sign, Haunts of Richmond, hangs out in front, moving slightly in the breeze. Inside, it is dark. There's a counter where one can purchase tickets with a wall behind it covered with T-shirts and other collectibles one can buy.

The owners are Scott and Sandi Bergman. Scott has always loved going to haunted house attractions. His parents always took him and his three siblings to them at Halloween. After he grew up and went to school on a theatre scholarship, he met and married Sandi. Both went to London. While there, they visited the London Dungeon. Coming back, they found the building at N. 18th Street and started the Haunts of Richmond. The building they use was built in 1868.

At first, it was only a haunted house where they presented true local ghost stories, using actors to portray the characters. But people kept calling and asking about the ghost tours. Sandi told them it was a haunted house museum only. But finally, after so many requests, they started doing the ghost tours.

I remember how popular both were the weekend before Halloween in 2005, as crowds of people lined up to purchase tickets for both the haunted house and the tours. Our tour left the building through Shockoe Bottom, led by one of two guides. Our first stop was the building that had been

Castle Thunder Prison during the Civil War. From there, the tour stopped next at the Flood Wall. After that, we headed up toward the State Capitol and Governor's Mansion, finally circling back down Broad Street toward the Bottom, pausing along the way for the guide to tell a few more tales.

Haunts of Richmond Building.

The tour ended back at the Haunts of Richmond. If you visit, be sure to wear your best walking shoes—you'll get a workout. Sandi says that they only do the longer tours in warmer weather now.

Even more interesting is the fact that Haunts of Richmond building has its own ghost. Last year, one of the actors claimed to have seen it. No one else had seen the ghost and discredited the sighting at first. But when the local Richmond radio station, *Q-94*, broadcasted from there on Halloween, they brought a psychic, Patrick Matthews, with them. He was there for call-ins from listeners, taking questions. Between eight and eight-thirty am that morning, though—with all the lights on—suddenly, Patrick put a hand to his throat. He told Sandi that they had a ghost there, that she had been strangled in that building, and that her name was Mary.

Now they realized that maybe they shouldn't have discredited the actor's story so quickly. After that, other actors came forth and admitted to experiencing weird phenomena. There is a door in the long passageway they use for the haunted house, that looks like part of the wall—the actors use it to enter or exit. From time to time, it would swing open and no one would be back there. Sometimes, an actor would feel someone walk by and think that maybe it was Scott, but discovering afterwards that it wasn't, or that Scott was in front of them all the time.

Sandi Bergman, conducting a Haunts of Richmond Ghost Tour, October 21, 2006.

Two actors confirmed this, backing each other up word for word. Even customers mention that their hair has been played with while going through the haunted house and they knew it wasn't an actor, as they are not allowed to touch the people. Actors or others sometimes think that someone passing them is merely an actor dressed in black, only to discover no one was there. And one night, an actor came out, drained of all color, saying that he actually saw the ghostly Mary.

Sandi admits to never having seen a ghost herself—thinks they're creepy, in fact. But now she can use their own ghost as advertisement for their attraction. After all, how many places like theirs have a real bona fide haunt?

State Capitol (being renovated at the time).

The Terrible Catastrophe at the State Capitol

Surrounded by fences while it's being renovated, Virginia's Capitol building remains looking like one of the ancient Greek temples. It is just as imposing, too. But in the dark of night, one swears that the cries for help and screams of horror rend the air.

Though it had served as the Capitol of the Confederacy, it escaped any damage. But on April 27, 1870, its luck ran out. Minutes before the Virginia Supreme Court of Appeals convened, a loud cracking noise resounded, followed by pandemonium. The gallery floor collapsed under the hundreds of spectators and participants who had crowded into the room earlier. Bodies, bricks, iron bars, planks, and furniture fell to the courtroom below. This caused that floor to buckle, and everything continued down to the ground floor some forty feet below.

Many were crushed to death, others suffocated from the huge cloud of dust that arose. Still others were buried alive under all the rubble. The lucky ones who managed to escape, ran, walked, and crawled their way outside.

Firemen, police, and others came to the rescue, but it took hours to dig through the mess and find the tangled-up bodies. Survivors carried to the lawn looked like 'bloody ghosts' more than human beings. When word got out, wives, relatives, and friends rushed to the scene, adding to the chaos.

Sixty-two men died—ten less than the ghastly theatre fire in 1811. More than 250 had been injured, some permanently. Victims included prominent citizens like Patrick Henry's grandson. Luckily, the House of Delegates hadn't been in session at the time, otherwise the tragedy could have been worse. Strangely, the judges for the Supreme Court of Appeals escaped. They had delayed proceedings as they talked over some changes in their written opinion of a case and were about to go back in when the tragedy struck. They found themselves overlooking a terrible abyss.

With the capitol city plunged into mourning, there were decisions to be made. Should the Capitol building be demolished and a new one built? It was decided that the existing building was to be rebuilt and refortified.

More than a century has passed since that terrible time. Some say eerie cries can still be heard within the Capitol.

Virginia's Governor Shares His Mansion with Ghosts

Constructed in 1813, the Governor's Mansion is an elegant, stately place—an old Southern gentlewoman that has only improved with age. Downtown, it has been called a wonderful example of Federal style architecture and is the symbol of Virginia itself.

A four-room wooden house that housed earlier governors once stood where today's Mansion stands. The house had become downtrodden and was torn down to make way for the new building. Boston architect Alexander Parris had been commissioned to draw up plans for the Mansion. But those plans weren't thought to reflect what the state really meant, and others added their own ideas to it.

A big mistake.

Many people didn't like the result. It was called inferior and almost a discredit to the Commonwealth by one Richmond newspaper, who added that the exterior was "one of the homeliest dwellings in the city." But these criticisms were kind compared to what one of the later governors' wives said about it. She said it had: "a tin roof, ugly floors, and copper bathtubs," and that the carpets hadn't been taken up for forty years. If that wasn't bad enough, a visiting chairman of the General Assembly Finance Committee sat down in a gilt chair and it splintered beneath him. Embarrassed, because he was a large man, he tried to hide the pieces in a potted palm.

It had improvements, eventually. One of the governors, James Barbour, had balustrades added along the eaves and railed in four Georgian chimneys to make a "captain's walk." Other additions included porticos so that the south and north entrances looked more inviting. The tin roof was replaced by a slate one, and the copper bathtubs were replaced with porcelain. An oval dining room was put in, the outdoor kitchen was moved into the basement, and a ballroom was made by joining two back rooms. Along with a library, study, breakfast room, more wonderful furnishings were added over the years that ranged from Hepplewhites to Duncan Phyfes. A vast collection of paintings, portraits, porcelains, figurines, and silver service completed the Mansion.

Five U. S. Presidents had visited, along with Winston Churchill, Queen Elizabeth, Charles Lindbergh, King Edward VII, and Admiral Richard E. Byrd. Four future presidents lived there, and General Stonewall Jackson laid in state there in 1863.

Besides the living, there's another occupant, or maybe just a visitor to the Mansion—a spectral one. The first sighting, in the early 1890s, appeared to none other than Governor Philip W. McKinney.

One hot and humid afternoon in August, Governor McKinney entered the Mansion. He washed up in the bathroom, walked into one of the bedrooms, and was startled to find a young lady at the window. Wondering who she was, he left and found his wife, asking who their guest was. His wife replied that she didn't have any guest. McKinney went back to the bedroom, only to discover the young woman gone. A search ensued, but she was never found, or any clues as to who she was—or had been.

Another time, she was seen by a member of the Capitol police force. The officer noticed her standing by the curtains of an upstairs bedroom, where unauthorized guests were not allowed. Just as he walked over to her to tell her to leave, she dissipated before his eyes.

The ghost has been known to be heard, too, and once felt. Footsteps would echo in the Mansion when no one but the security officer was in the building. Servants heard the woman walking, the sounds of her taffeta dress rustling along with the footsteps. A butler once chased her down into the basement, where she vanished.

Many times she would be heard by security, as they sat around a table in the kitchen hallway in the basement. Always the sounds came from upstairs, doors slamming and footsteps echoing. One officer went up to check it out, finding all the doors locked tight and no one around.

When Governor Andrew Montague was in office, Dr. Horace Hoskins and Robert Lynch lived in the Mansion. Both had been awakened one night by the sounds of someone walking in a silk skirt inside their room. They followed the sound out of their room, along the corridor, and down the hallway until the sound disappeared. The Official Mansion Tour script reported that, like the butler who had chased the ghost, so did Governor Montague's brother—right out into the street!

In 1972, during Governor Linwood Holton's tenure, when Hurricane Agnes tore through Richmond, a blackout occurred that affected both the Capitol and the Governor's Mansion. It was dark everywhere in the city, except for one light bulb in the ladies stairwell of the Mansion that stayed lit during the storm. Ann Compton, *ABC-TV*'s White House correspondent then, who happened to be on assignment at the state Capitol, said the light switches were flipped on and off, but it didn't seemed to affect it; the light just kept on shining. As reported in the *Richmond Times-Dispatch* later, Governor Holton made mention that someone moved several of the paintings in his bedroom during the storm.

Governor's Mansion.

One Capitol policeman actually was scared so much, he left his job. This officer was in the basement one night when something touched his face. Terrified, he ran out of the Mansion, giving his badge back and quitting, only coming back to get his last paycheck. Another officer during Governor Dalton's tenure caught the governor's dog barking at a window. The room had a sudden drop in temperature, becoming frigid, and though it was summertime, the window's glass frosted over. The curtains moved, then stilled, and the frost on the glass disappeared.

Another spirit seen at the Mansion is one of a butler. The officer who saw him turned around and noticed a tall, thin African American dressed all in black and wearing white gloves. He carried a full-service tea tray. The butler walked away, into what had been the old kitchen, and the officer followed him. When the officer entered the kitchen, he found no one there.

No one has ever discovered who the young lady was, or even the butler. Whether tied to the Mansion, or possibly there before it was built, could the lady just like the look of the place and want to visit? As for the butler, did he feel that his duties weren't over, even after death? Whatever the case may be, the governors and their families share the Governor's Mansion with these two spectral inhabitants.

Haunted
Shockoe Bottom

Haunts of Richmond is not the only building in Shockoe Bottom with its own ghost. Many other places in the Bottom have reported ghostly phenomena. If one could take the time to ask at all the stores, bars, restaurants, and homes in the area, no doubt there would be a wealth of specter activity. With a long, illustrious history behind the Bottom and nearby Shockoe Slip, this part of the city could be one of the most haunted areas in Richmond.

The Laser Quest Building

One place where one *wouldn't* expect anything of the supernatural kind is the Laser Quest building, which stands back-to-back with the Haunts of Richmond building. But once one realizes what the building was used for in 1860-61, the reason for the haunting becomes clear. Once upon a time it was a Civil War hospital.

When you walk into the place, you find a room with a desk where people can sign up to play Laser Quest. The main floor is where you play the game, but upstairs are the offices. It is up there that Confederate soldiers have been seen walking down the hall, and where cold spots pop up so suddenly—freezing cold.

Laser Quest Building.

Downstairs, in a room just to your right upon entering the building, is a circle of bloodspots on the stone floor, just under the window. There's an equipment room kept locked, for obvious reasons, and many of the monitors who are there to watch the games will suddenly see it open by itself. There's a known rule that anyone walking out of one of the offices must first whistle, as a signal to others there. Without that whistle, no one will leave an office; for no whistle and the sound of footsteps means that a ghost, and not a living person, walks the halls. One worker felt a chilly spot suddenly at the desk where she worked. It was freezing cold and she felt overcome with anxiety, growing tense. She got up to leave for a bit. When she returned, the cold spot was gone and she felt okay again. Though the name of the spirit is unknown, they call it Beauregard.

The Haunted Pub, McCormicks

In the Irish pub across the street from Haunts of Richmond, McCormick's has their own little spirit, and not the kind found in their alcoholic beverages. They hear audio equipment upstairs fall down with a crash, and when they rush up to see what has happened, they find nothing wrong. In a separate room, they hear something fall, like glass breaking, but upon going into that room, nothing is ever disturbed.

The Haunted Richbrau

Richbrau, in nearby Shockoe Slip, is where they brew beers and have both a bar and a restaurant. But those working there think that a brothel once stood on the exact spot Richbrau's now occupies. And it seems that the ladies of the evening are still there—still trying to drum up business.

People have seen women walking around when they shouldn't be there. Six people told Sandi Bergman of Haunts of Richmond that they heard their names called out. One even admitted to someone whispering into his ear, but when he turned around, he found no one behind him.

There are two padlocks on one of the main doors; the other one has a combination lock. One day, one of the padlocks turned up missing, and though they searched everywhere, it couldn't be found. Not worried as they had the combination to the door, they locked up and left for the night. The next day when they returned, both padlocks hung on the door as always. Just after that, locks of all kinds started appearing.

Since they brew beer there and don't want just anyone to get inside to steal any of it, they always keep the beer room locked. The key is kept downstairs, and one day the assistant manager couldn't find it in the place where it was always kept. He searched the whole building, joined by several others. They double-checked the original location and knew it definitely wasn't there. But after some hours of searching, they found it, right back where it was always hung.

Big Daddy's

Another bar called Big Daddy's is haunted, too. Built in the 1870s, it is one of the oldest spots in the city. It started life as a furniture store, with the downstairs as the store and the upstairs the family's home. Later, it became a dry goods store, and for the last few years, a succession of bars has inhabited the building, with Big Daddy's being the latest.

Before they opened Big Daddy's, the place was remodeled. Even then, there were occurrences. When the rooms were being painted, the painters had the radio on two rooms away. Suddenly, the radio would change channels for no reason whatsoever. Other times, they would come back the next day and find one of the doors on the second floor opened when they knew they had locked it securely the night before. At first, they thought someone was breaking into the place. One day, when they came in and heard the door to the women's restroom upstairs being opened, they rushed up, hoping to catch the person. But there was no one there, or anywhere else in the building.

Bernard experiences a lot of the phenomena. One time, as he was washing dishes, he had to leave for a few minutes. He left the clean dishes stacked up on one side of the sink and the dirty ones on the other side. When he came back he found all of the clean ones spread out. Just then he heard someone walking behind him, and when he turned around, he saw no one.

It is the opinion of those who work in Big Daddy's that the ghost is either the daughter, or the wife, of the family who owned the furniture store.

Rosie Connolly's Irish Pub and Restaurant

Rosie Connolly's is an Irish pub and restaurant on 1548A East Main Street, located on one side of the Farmer's Market. A place that has exceptional Irish stew; it makes you feel as if you're in a pub in Ireland or England, with sixties music piped in as you have a pint of Guinness. The restaurant and the pub are brand new, but where the kitchen is, once stood the YMCA. And that's where the ghost has been seen. The owner, Tommy Goulding, admitted that once he had been in the kitchen and kept feeling that someone was watching him. But he has never seen the ghost.

Some of the waitresses have seen the spirit. One waitress who used to work there turned around and saw the apparition. She said he looked like he was wearing blue coveralls or a tunic. She later resigned and went back to Louisiana. Another waitress also saw him one day, and said it appeared he was wearing denim coveralls or a tunic. For anyone wanting great Irish beer or food, check out their website at: http://www/rosieconnollys.com.

Main Street Station

Originally built in 1901, Main Street Station was a train station which operated until the 1970s, and then was closed down. It reopened a couple of years ago to become a functioning train depot once more. But more than people rush to catch trains in this depot. There's a parlor there with the men's room on one side and the women's on the other. It is mainly in the women's room, and sometimes the parlor, that the ghostly phenomenon occurs.

When it was being remodeled and the asbestos removed, the supervisor found he could not schedule a late night shift starting at midnight because people would often call in sick. The crew chief told him that no one wanted to work because of "too many things walking around." One time, when a ladder was propped up against the wall, footsteps were heard on the fourth floor. Because no one was supposed to be in the station other than the workers, they went up to search, and found no one. When they came back down, they discovered the ladder folded up and lying on the ground.

One of the women who worked there entered the women's restroom, and while she was using the toilet, heard another one flush in another stall. Next she heard footsteps, and then the faucets of one of the sinks being turned on and poured water. She stepped out and found no one in the restroom with her at all.

A janitor once waited to mop the floor of the women's restroom, since he could hear someone walking around inside. After forty-five minutes, worried about the person still there and thinking that maybe there was a problem, he knocked and peeked in. The room was empty.

Passengers mention from time to time that they have heard someone walking around in the women's restroom, as well.

1 West Main Street

A famous resident of Shockoe Bottom was author Ellen Glasgow. Born in 1873, Ellen was a member of a prominent family of Richmond; she was engaged twice but never married. She wrote twenty novels, and lived in the family home at 1 West Main Street until her death. After her death, owners of the home heard the buzzer system going off when it was no longer connected. Upstairs, in the room she must have used in life, a typewriter can be heard—when one enters the room, the sound halts, but starts up again when the person leaves. Workers tearing down the row of stone houses across the street from the Glasgow home have heard the heart-wrenching wails of a woman crying in the house, though it was empty at the time.

Julep's New Southern Cuisine

Julep's New Southern Cuisine restaurant at 1721 E. Franklin Street has more than fine food; it has its own interesting history and haunting. Beginning life as a lumber house in 1817, in 1832, it became a weapons shop owned by gunsmith James McNaught. McNaught had an apprentice, Daniel Denoon, who after a while, wanted to go out on his own. He had been afraid to do so because McNaught had a bad temper, but finally, at age twenty, he walked upstairs and said, "I'm going, and leaving on my own."

McNaught, angry, grabbed a pistol and shot Daniel from the top of the stairs. Daniel fell down the steps, dead. Shortly after, McNaught was arrested. Three days later, in prison, he was found strangled by a silk scarf. No one knew how the scarf got inside his cell.

At Julep's, there still can be heard the sounds of a body falling down the stairs to the floor, just under the bottom step.

Stone House

The oldest stone building in Richmond is the Stone House, which houses the Edgar Allan Poe Museum—even though Poe never visited the house. The museum docents suspect that the former children of the original family that owned the home in the 1730s, are the spectral children seen playing around the property from time to time. That family was led by Samuel Edge, who had prospered in flour, the second biggest export after tobacco.

In the back of the museum, when people reach over the privacy fence to take pictures of the windows there, occasionally a face will show up in the picture. Sometimes, one of the workers will come in for the day, and when they head upstairs, they find a little boy sitting on the floor, looking out the window. Before their eyes, he dissipates. Other times, sounds of crashing coming from upstairs can be heard, and the museum docents race up to find things scattered across the floor—but no one around.

Then there's the garden out back. Tourists with video recorders come back inside and ask who the children they captured playing in the garden are. When they playback the video, a boy and a girl are playing, exactly as they have said. On those occasions, however, there were no children there to be recorded. There have also been people who've made a sweep with their video cameras only to find that when they get to the house, the screen goes blank, coming back on again when the camera passes it.

Castle Thunder Prison

Castle Thunder Prison is located in Shockoe Bottom, at the end of 18th Street, not far from the Flood Wall. A former tobacco warehouse located on Tobacco Row, it had been converted into a prison used by the Confederacy to house civilian prisoners. It housed captured Union spies, political prisoners, and others charged with treason during the Civil War. A large number of its inmates were under sentence of death. Even though the inmates were sometimes allowed boxes of medicine and other supplies, the prison guards had a reputation for brutality—these items never reached the intended.

Among its many notable occupants was Union officer William Jackson Palmer (1836-1909). In 1862, he was captured in civilian clothes while scouting before the Battle of Antietam within Confederate lines, gathering information for General George McClellan. When questioned, he gave his name as W. J. Peters, and claimed to be a mine owner on an inspection trip. While the Confederates did not know he was a spy, his circumstances were suspicious, and he was detained. He was set free in a prisoner exchange and rejoined his Regiment in February 1863.

After the Union forces captured Richmond, they used the prison for similar purposes. Among those known to have been incarcerated there in this later period was Mollie Bean, a woman who had served for two years in the 47th North Carolina Infantry and was twice wounded in action. She had pretended to be man in order to get into the Confederate Army, but her Union captors suspected her of being a spy.

With such an illustrious past, especially the brutality and severe punishment, this is a place that was sure to become haunted. Sandi Bergman of Haunts of Richmond said that everything she had heard about it, ghostwise, had been second hand. That included sounds of ghostly footsteps and stuff being moved. And yet, when I took a photograph of it with my digital camera, I saw flickering striped light in the viewfinder in one of the windows of the prison that reminded me of the window of the lab in the old Frankenstein's Monster movie from the '30s, or the kind of lighting a disco ball displays.

My husband looked through the viewfinder, too, and he said that he saw the effect as well. However, when we looked up at the building, all we saw were the normal, dark windows—with all appearances that the prison was empty. The sky was overcast, the time was between 5:30 and 6:00 PM, with no sunlight shining down. Later, after I'd snapped two photos of the building, we saw that same peculiar window looking as if a full shutter or blinds covered it; plus, two other windows looked lit up when, at the time, they certainly were not. I can't explain it. At the time, it felt very creepy—and yet at the same time, exciting—for something like that to happen. A first-hand ghostly experience!

Castle Thunder Prison with the weird windows phenomenon.

The Mystery Sword of the Masonic Hall

There's one last story to tell. It's a quaint story about the oldest Masonic Hall in the United States, located in Shockoe Bottom, though it's not a ghost story. It seems that, just after the Civil War, a meeting was held in the Masonic Hall, and when it was dispersed, a sword was discovered. But no one came forward to claim it. The Free Masons still have it to this day-- waiting for someone to come and claim it. In an area teeming with ghostly phenomenon, is there a more spooky reason for its mysterious presence? We may never know ...

A Prophecy and a
Terrible Fire

Richmond Theatre once stood on the north side of Broad Street between 12th and College. It caught fire on December 26, 1811, resulting in tragedy. There's not only a ghost story connected to it, but one of prophecy, too.

A chilling tale came to light about 100 years afterwards, in an unpublished monograph written by a Mrs. Nannie Dunlop Werth, found in the archives of the Virginia Historical Society in Richmond. The story was about Mrs. Werth's grandmother, Mrs. McRae, who happened to be at the fire that night. The story also concerned Mr. and Mrs. Patrick Gibson's young ward, Nancy Green. One day short of her sixteenth birthday on December 26, 1811, Nancy had a psychic experience.

Mrs. Gibson had wanted the girl to go to the theater that evening, but Nancy refused. They finally managed to convince her to go, when Mrs. Gibson said that it showed proper respect for her to do so.

That afternoon, Mrs. Gibson sent Nancy off to make a purchase on Broad Street. Passing 8th Street as she crossed the ravine, something chanted out to her, "Nancy, Nancy, Nancy Green, you'll die before you are sixteen."

Frightened, she related it to Mrs. Werth's grandmother, who happened to live across from Nancy's guardians' home. Nancy still went ahead with Mrs. McRae, Mrs. Gibson, and others to see the play, *The Bleeding Nun.*

The *Richmond Enquirer* reported that the play, a comic-pantomime, brought in an audience of 600, making it the fullest house of the season. The audience held some of the most distinguished, cultured, and refined people, including Governor George Smith. The play went off without a hitch. Then, after the beginning of the second act, something happened. Backstage, one of the players ordered a young boy to raise a chandelier of open, lighted candles. But the boy warned that if he did, the scenery might catch fire. Still, they commanded him to hoist the chandelier up.

As he did, the fire leaped to the scenery. He gave the alarm in the rear of the stage, telling some of the attendants to cut the cords of the combustible materials. But the person asked to do this became panic stricken and took off. All this happened while one of the actors performed near the orchestra, and the fire was obscured from the audience by a curtain.

The flames spread quickly, and the fire fell from the ceiling upon the performer. For the first time, the people in the audience became aware of the danger. With cries of fire in the air, people left their seats and bolted for the lobbies and stairs. Wives screamed for their husbands and children shrieked as the place filled with flames and choking amounts of smoke. Many got trodden underfoot, while others were thrown back from the windows from which they tried to leap. Many did jump from the windows of the first story and were saved, but others ended up on the ground below, with broken legs and thighs, and more.

The fire was fully evolved now, and some people of color in the gallery who escaped down the stairs, were cut off from the rest of the house. Some, who didn't find a loved one or friend among those who escaped, plunged back into the burning building and perished. The Governor, along with other gentlemen, shared this fate attempting to rescue others. In a book published a half century later, Samuel Mordecai told of a physician, Dr. James D. Mc-Caw and an African-American blacksmith, Gilbert Hunt, who rescued some of those caught inside. Dr. McCaw told Gilbert to stand below a window where he'd broken the glass, and to catch anyone dropped from above. James seized the woman nearest to him and lowered her from the window as low as he could, then let her drop. Gilbert caught her and handed her over to others. One after another, the doctor kept doing this, passing the victims to Gilbert. They managed to save ten to twelve ladies.

After rescuing all within his reach, James tried to save himself. With the wall already tottering, he attempted to drop down himself, but his leather gaiter caught on a hinge or some other iron projection. It suspended him in a horrible and painful way. He did manage to get loose and fell to the ground, ending up lame for life. His muscles and sinews torn and lacerated, and his back burned, he carried those marks to his death.

An editor who attended the play wrote: "Alas, gushing tears and unspeakable anguish deprive me of utterance. No tongue can tell—no pen or pencil can describe—the woeful catastrophe. No person, who was not present, can form any idea of the unexplained scene of human distress."

As for Nancy Green, she did die as prophesied. Only Mrs. McRae and two others in their party survived. As reported by Mrs. Werth in her article: "Mrs. McRae was pacing up and down the aisle of the second balcony, then the dress circle, suffocating under a heavy burden of smoke, when she was attracted to a nearby window by a burning fragment which fell from the cornice above. She rushed frantically forward seeking fresh air and leaned out. A man's voice cried, "Jump, I'll catch you." Knowing it was certain death to disregard the call; she sprang into strong arms and was saved."

But Nancy Green never escaped. Neither did her guardian. As prophesized, Nancy did die before she turned sixteen. Seventy-two people in total perished, while countless others were injured.

As was written in the newspaper at the time: "The morning sun rose over the ashes of the Chief Executive of the Commonwealth, and the highest and lowest of the people, mingled in an indistinguishable smoldering mass. The holy season for joy and gladness was, to the awe-struck community, one of lamentation and of weeping, of deep and bitter sorrow. The state, indeed the whole country, mourned in sincere sympathy, with afflicted Richmond."

The day after the tragedy, December 27, 1811, the Common Council of Richmond passed an ordinance. Any remains not claimed by relatives would be collected into urns, coffins, and other suitable enclosures and buried on the public burying ground. A tomb, or tombs, were to be erected over them as approved, with such inscriptions that would best record the "melancholy and afflicting event." The ordinance also stated that citizens keep their shops, counting houses, and offices closed for forty-eight hours after the passing of the ordinance. For a term of four months, no one could exhibit any public show or spectacle, or open any public dancing assembly within the city. Anyone who did, was penalized, and had to pay six dollars and sixty-six cents for every hour should such be exhibited. A day of humiliation and prayer had been also set aside, "that the citizens wear crepe for a month."

The original burial site was to be at St. John's Church on Richmond Hill, but later, changed to the theatre site. As described in the *Richmond Enquirer,* the funeral procession moved up Capitol Hill to the devoted spot. With the whole city in attendance, crying erupted as the burial went forward, the remains put all together in one common grave.

Seven months after the fire, a young architect named Robert Mills laid the cornerstone of Monumental Church. Completed in 1814, it is now considered one of the nation's major architectural landmarks, and not only the grandest, but the only remaining example of the five octagonal, domed churches that Mills designed. The building is covered in funeral details and has references to the fire. The capitals of the two columns feature upside-down torches and stars and drapes that are surrounded by a flame-like carving on a pediment as symbols of mourning.

This church may also be the basis for Edgar Allan Poe's, "The Fall of the House of Usher," as a couple named Usher preformed at the theater. One of them even knew Poe's actress mother. As a youth, Poe attended the church. A bit of an ironic side note: Poe's mother died two weeks before the fire, too.

The knowledge that one may be standing upon a grave and the gloominess of the building has one listening for moans, screams, and scratching at the walls. Instead, there is only ethereal silence. Maybe the victims have been appeased with the erection of the tomb that shelters them.

And so it seems that the true ghost story attached to the fire is the one about the prophecy that happened before it and the demise of young Nancy Green.

Monumental Church.

The Train
Under the Hill

Haunts of Richmond tells this story on its Ghost Walk, and it is famous—a part of Richmond's interesting past. It is the tale of the Church Hill Tunnel located at Jefferson Park Hill, above Marshall and 19th Streets.

The Chesapeake and Ohio railroad decided to build a tunnel through the hill instead of routing the train around Richmond. It was roughly estimated to cost $1.1 million at the time to do so; the objective was to improve rail access to Richmond from the east. When completed, the tunnel would measure around 4,000 feet long, making it one of the longest tunnels in the county at the time. But its usage was short-lived, for in 1902, an elevated railroad viaduct along the James River opened up, making the Church Hill Tunnel unnecessary. A cave-in occurred with six houses in Jefferson Park collapsing into the tunnel. The Chesapeake and Ohio Railroad reportedly celebrated its closure and that seemed to be the end of it at the time.

By 1925, the railroad viaduct hit capacity, and the officials felt they needed to run more trains through the city, so city officials reopened the Church Hill Tunnel. And on October 2, 1925, the railroad decided to go ahead with the railroad tunnel, ignoring its earlier fate. Railroad engineers cleaned and inspected the tunnel, then reopened it. Brickwork and drainage ditches were reinforced along the tunnel walls.

On a rainy Friday afternoon, a black laborer named Lemy Campbell worked near one of the entrances to the tunnel. Inside, a group of men worked, doing tunnel repairs, while engineer Tom Mason sat inside the cab of a work train locomotive, Engine 231, used to switch cars. Just after three o'clock in the afternoon, Campbell heard a brick fall, then another and another. A terrible crackling noise sounded along the tunnel roof and he dashed for safety. The roof crashed down behind him. The combined sounds of earth, bricks, timber, and the screams of trapped men were loud and horrifying. Lights in the tunnel flickered and went out, and crew members and laborers rushed for the exits. Some did make it out of the western entrance, which was only a few hundred yards away, but the others scrambled for the eastern one, nearly a mile away. In the darkness, panic went wild.

One survivor mentioned to the *Richmond Times Dispatch* that men passed him screaming and fighting. Some of them yelled that they had knives and would cut anyone that got in their way. Praying, losing their way in the dark, butting their heads into the walls, they fell over tires and knocked each other down. It has been described as being in a bottomless pit.

Engineer Mason became trapped in the cab. Fireman B. F. Mosby managed to crawl underneath ten flat cars and escaped the tunnel, only to die that night from burns he received from the steam of the locomotive. The conductor, C. G. McFadden, along with brakeman C. S. Kelso, made it out. Another brakeman, A.G. Adams, though knocked to the ground and stunned by the avalanche of dirt, managed to make it to daylight. It took hours before an accounting of the laborers could be made, and it was claimed that two had been buried alive in the tunnel.

The rescue attempts continued for about nine days, hampered by fresh cave-ins. On Sunday, October 11th, they managed to dig through and find the upright body of the engineer locked in by the brake, crushed to death.

Worse, afterwards, smaller cave-ins shifted homes and even gobbled part of a park.

Questions and legends abound about this tragedy even today. Are the two black laborers still buried in that tunnel? And were they wrong, and more than four people killed in the disaster? Many survivors reported that several other laborers had just been taken in for that day's work. How many people were unaccounted for in reality? The place was filled with sand; the two entrances are sealed off and hidden behind a growth of trees and vines.

A legend that connected this event to the 'Vampire' of Hollywood Cemetery came about when the one man who had survived was taken later to a hospital. Having gotten mixed up in the vampire legend as being some kind of fiend that dug his way out of the tunnel, it was said that he ran all the way back to the mausoleum where he, as the vampire, was buried, while being pursued by an angry mob.

For a long time, there were no ghost stories attached to the tragedy. But as Sandi of Haunts of Richmond said, "Yes, there is." A man on one of her tours told her that he had worked at Richmond Cold Storage, the white building in front of the hill. He worked the graveyard shift and would hear the sounds of pickaxes coming from the hill.

One young man, who went to Virginia Commonwealth University, along with some friends, approached the hill one night when they heard the sound of air brakes coming from inside it! They knew it wasn't from some modern train as they looked back at the tracks several blocks behind them and saw nothing. My husband said that it had to be the sound of steam, as it was a steam engine buried under the hill, and wouldn't have the air brakes of a modern train.

The third story attached to this tragedy has to do with the park at the top of Church Hill. People claim they can hear cries for help coming from inside the hill itself.

Last summer, in 2006, funded workers started to dig down into the tunnel, hoping to unearth the train. The search team, led by Gulf and Ohio Railways CEO and Chairman Pete Clausen, began digging in June, but was ordered to stop working in July. City officials were concerned about the stability of the hill above the tunnel. Also, they had told workers to stop pumping water from the tunnel over the weekend, when they realized the excavation team had not applied for permits or submitted a water disposal plan to the city. Richmond Mayor Doug Wilder's spokesman, Linwood Norman, says the need for permits seemed to have been overlooked. And so the train is still buried beneath the hill. ... As are the ghostly workers, too ...

Byrd Theatre Has More than Movies

The aroma of freshly popped popcorn permeates the theater. And not just popcorn, but good popcorn! Voted in Richmond's Style Weekly Magazine as the best theatre popcorn in the city, Byrd Theater's popcorn deserves the praise. As a second-run movie theatre, it shows films that have already gone through the other first-run theatres. A grand place, elegant and refined, the theater is like a lady who has aged well. One wouldn't think of ghosts, except maybe from memories of all the movies past.

One can visualize its grand opening. Women in flapper dresses on the arms of gentlemen pass through the doors to enter the theatre, edgy with excitement, to see Waterfront, a silent film that was the first movie ever shown there.

Located in Carytown, nestled among shops, restaurants, art galleries, and more in a twelve-block shopping area that extends along Cary Street from the Powhite Parkway to the Boulevard, the Byrd Theatre was designed by the architect Fred Bishop in the French Empire style. Bishop also designed many other theatres and buildings, including the Arlington Theatre in Arlington, Virginia.

Built by Walter Coulter and Charles Somma, and the first of its kind to be equipped with a sound system, this 1400-seat theater opened on December 24, 1928. The first audiences paid fifty cents for the evening shows and twenty-five cents for the matinees, while children were admitted for only a dime. Though the balcony was originally built with the intention of accommodating blacks during segregation, the theater did not open its doors to the African-American population until the 1960s. If any colored person came to the theater before the sixties, he or she would be given admission and cab fare to any of the black theaters in the city—among them the Hippodrome on 2nd Street and the Empire on Broad.

Decorated with murals of Greek myths, the theatre also has imported Greek and Italian marble, crystal chandeliers, hand-sewn velvet drapes, and fountains. It even has a central vacuum system. There's a Wurlitzer—still played today by organist Bob Gulledge every Saturday night. A natural underground spring is in the basement, and no, the water pumped from it is not used by the building's air conditioning system. Designated a state landmark in 1978, a year later, it also became a National Historic Landmark. The most remarkable thing about the Byrd is that it has somehow survived the past seventy years largely unaltered, both in appearance and function, and still shows movies to this day. An organization called the Byrd Theatre Foundation is trying to raise money to buy the theatre and keep it going. From the Byrd Theatre's website: "In an effort to insure the continued vitality of the Byrd as a movie theatre and entertainment venue, the Byrd Foundation will purchase the building and business, converting it to a not-for-profit 501 3(c) entity." (It would be nice if they do, keeping this great place open for the generations to come.)

Its first manager was Robert Coulter, the son of one of the two builders, Walter Coulter. He managed the theatre from 1928 to 1971, and passed away not long after being forced to retire. Management was taken over by his assistant manager, George Stitzer. It is Robert Coulter who is believed to be the ghost who haunts the theatre.

Bill Enos works at the theatre. He knows his job well, along with a good knowledge of the theatre. His opinion on the footsteps, and the fact that some people have heard them, is that it is the acoustics of the place—and not really the footsteps of the ghost himself.

He did mention a story about an aspiring organist, Robert Lint, who has played the organ there. Lint returned one Saturday night, around 3:30 to 4 AM, to practice his playing on the organ. When he heard someone cough, sounding like it came from directly behind him, he turned around to see who it was and found no one was there. He resumed playing; fifteen minutes later, someone coughed again, and again he turned around and no one was there. He was the only one in the theatre at that time. It was then that he decided to quit and leave the theater.

Byrd Theatre Building.

Todd Schall-Vess is the current manager. He knew that the ghost was Robert Coulter from all the descriptions, but admits to having never seen or heard him. When asked when the ghost was first seen, he replied, "The earliest was the early '70s." He further said that the ghost was seen sitting in a theatre seat in the balcony. It had been a favorite seat of the former theatre manager when he was alive—and obviously still was after his death.

The ghost has also been witnessed by the projectionists, in the projection booth. Windows from the booth look out into the theater, and the shadow of "someone" would pass by them. The projectionist would turn around and find no one there. Todd says that whether it was Coulter's ghost, or someone else's, it's hard to tell from just a shadow. No one ever found out who or what the shadow belonged to.

Another place that Coulter had been seen is at the back doors after closing, when someone would be barring them. Suddenly, he'd appear to the person locking up, as if he was offering to help do the job, too.

The ghost seems to prefer to make appearances when the theater is dark and deserted, and others are not around—except for the person who has the experience. However, he had been spotted a time or two seeming to enjoy a movie with fellow movie-goers. These instances have been reported by employees and their friends who were allowed by Todd to go up to the balcony (normally blocked off) to watch a movie. They noticed the elderly gentlemen sitting in the seat Coulter preferred when he was alive. Afterwards they would ask Todd, "Who was that old man in the seat up there?" Obviously, the only answer: Coulter—as no one else is allowed up there.

There are stories online about the restrooms being reputedly haunted too. Another of many myths about the theater, Todd feels that people have gotten this confused with another tale from another theatre in Richmond, the Landmark. He says it happens all the time, and not just with the haunted restrooms either. People come to the theater and ask about the swimming pool, mistaking the underground spring for one. Of course, there is a theater in Richmond that does have a swimming pool, but it's not the Byrd. That, too, is the Landmark, which has a twenty-by-seventy foot pool.

Whether for the atmosphere due to the haunting, or, more likely, due to the colorful history behind it, this is the place to catch a movie, or enjoy listening to the organ music being played on Saturday nights. Check out the Byrd Theatre at its website at http://www.byrdtheatre.com for what's playing and the times of the movies being shown there that week.

And while you're there, buy a bag of their popcorn—after all; it's the best in Richmond. And maybe, just maybe, besides a good flick, you might catch a glimpse of the ghost.

**Seat Robert Coulter's
Spirit has been seen
in the seat on the left.**

Dooley Mansion in Maymont Park

Once owned by wealthy entrepreneur Major James Henry Dooley and his wife, Sallie May Dooley, this mansion is now part of Maymont Park in Richmond. In 1886, Dooley purchased a 94-acre dairy farm above the fall line of the James River and built his home on the land.

James Dooley shared in the unusually advantageous economic climate of this time, often referred to as the Gilded Age. He not only participated in the larger national arena, but also in the complex economic and political environment of the post-Reconstruction South. An active contributor to the recovery and growth of the South's economy, he achieved this through expansion of the railways, land development, and other business ventures. As central figures in the social, intellectual, and philanthropic life of their city, the Dooley's interests and activities extended beyond Virginia, and their cosmopolitan perspective reflected in their home, Maymont.

Everything, from the grounds to the interior of the mansion, reflected the Victorian era. Architect Edgerton S. Rogers combined the Romanesque Revival style with the picturesque Queen Anne for the Dooley residence. Built of massive sandstone and accented by pink granite columns, turrets, and towers rising from it, gave it a castle-like look. By 1893, the Dooleys were living in their 12,000 square-foot, 33-room home, which they named "May Mont," a name which combines Mrs. Dooley's maiden name and the Italian word for hill. Indoors, they decorated the rooms with furniture from that era, including a swan-shaped bed.

After Mrs. Dooley's death in 1925, the mansion was bequeathed to the City of Richmond, and within six months, opened to the public as a museum. The interiors and a large original collection remained relatively untouched until the beginning of the restoration in 1970.

It was during that restoration that strange things happened, and people working there felt a presence.

One of them was Ragan Reaves. Many times, checking the house before leaving for the day, she thought she saw a blonde woman in a light dress or wrapper standing at one of the third floor windows. But coming closer, she found no one.

Someone else, Bonnie Biggs, admitted to thinking she had startled someone when she entered the house in the mornings. Always locked tight at night when everyone left, there was no way for it to be someone substantial. A quick glimpse revealed the tip of a woman's skirt vanishing around a corner. Objects in the Swan room, Mrs. Dooley's bedroom, were found to be moved. Everyone was asked and they deny touching anything.

No one today, however, has experienced any such phenomenon. Obviously, Sallie May Dooley was just checking up on the restoration, maybe to be sure things were done to her satisfaction.

To find out about a tour of the mansion or just to enjoy the park, visit the mansion's website: http://www.maymont.org/.

Dooley's Mansion in Maymont Park.

Jackson Ward

Dr. C. A. Bryce, a practitioner of medicine, was called late one night to come to Jackson Ward to treat a patient there. Something strange happened when he and the man who called him walked by a house there.

From an article in the Sunday issue of the *Richmond Times-Dispatch*, January 23, 1921, Dr. Bryce said, "I noticed that after going a few blocks, he started to turn into another street leading away from the most direct route to the point from which we had started." Bryce asked why they were doing that and the other man gave the reply that he didn't like passing an old house in the next block at night. The man went on about it being haunted, though the man himself had never personally experienced any of the supernatural manifestations.

Bryce's interest was piqued and he asked the other if they couldn't walk by the house anyway. They arrived at it and glanced at the tall, old wooden building. Two bushy cedars stood in front of the porch, almost obstructing the sight from the lower windows. The front door of the deserted house stood half open and the sash was missing from the upper window. Bryce heard a gentle slamming of an inside door on the upper floor. A depression overpowered him at that particular moment.

Nothing happened then, but after treating his patient, Bryce decided to stop by on his way home—alone.

It was very late and the town was asleep. The moonlight had become completely obscured by a clouded sky. Dr. Bryce gazed at the open door and window for only a few minutes when he thought he saw a small, white object moving around the porch floor. Before he could make out what it was, it disappeared, and he concluded that he hadn't seen anything—it was most likely his own imagination.

After that, he passed the place several times, with nothing occurring. But two years later, when he walked by it, something inexplicable *did* happen—it was after one in the morning and something transpired that really unnerved him.

A thunderstorm had taken place earlier that night, but the clouds had shifted, and every now and then, the moon shone down between rifts of floating clouds. He stood outside the house just as the moonlight fell upon the door and windows, and casting his eyes toward the sashes in the upper story, he saw a young girl's face. She was clad in only her night clothes, and the wind waved through her hair as it blew through the open sash.

He knew what he saw—the features were clear and distinct—a face he could recall years later. Suddenly, the apparition vanished and he never saw it again.

Wanting to make sure it wasn't a living being; the next day Bryce took a friend to explore the house. He wrote that it appeared deserted; looking like no human being had been in it for a long time, because of the layers of dust that lay undisturbed in every room.

Bryce couldn't offer a rational explanation for what he had seen, but neither would he call it a ghost. His opinion was that the face was not the work of his imagining mind, but a picture thrown upon his retina at some former time and reproduced in memory, or then and there, perceived from some substance on the window.

He managed to find out from the neighbors that three foreigners had lived there for a short time some years before, keeping mainly to themselves. They had departed abruptly without a word to anyone.

Five years later, he learned more about the house's history. When he called upon on a sick, old black man who lived in a cabin in the rear of the lot adjacent to the deserted house, Bryce recognized him from treating him several years before. The old man had paid him with a gold French coin, very unusual, and wouldn't explain where he'd gotten it.

When Bryce prodded him about the former occupants of the old house, the old man was reluctant to speak at first. Finally, with some coaxing on Bryce's part, he talked.

It seemed that years ago there were only acres of cornfields where the houses and streets now were. Three or four big frame houses stood out in the middle of these fields— the deserted house was one of them. The old man had been a boy then, and the house was only vacant and closed for a year or two when, one day, he noticed people in it: a gentleman, his wife, their daughter, and three women servants.

The old man's mother lived in the cabin then. After the new people moved in, a lady came down to ask his mother if she'd like to be employed to work in the house. And not only did they hire his mother, but him, as well. Foreign, they spoke in a language that neither the old man nor his mother understood, but the women servants who came with them could.

They never went out much, though sometimes they would send for a carriage and be driven out—mostly at night. The house was beautifully furnished and the family always dressed in fine clothing and plenty of jewelry. The young lady, Josephine, was very pretty. She would often take long walks by herself.

One day, the father called the old man to his room and asked, "Petaire [his name was Peter, but the man always called him Petaire], have you seen any man walking with my daughter any time?"

Peter gave the reply that he hadn't, and suspected from that questioning, that trouble was brewing. Later, he did see Josephine with a handsome, finely dressed man in Capitol Square, speaking a language he didn't understand. No doubt they were lovers.

Not long after, the man came to the house. Josephine met him at the door herself and begged him to leave before he was seen, but her father came to the door and invited him in. They argued, and the man left soon after. The other servants told Peter's mother hat he had demanded satisfaction as he left, and her father said he would meet him in New Orleans. She was told that this meant a duel.

A few days later, the father left, and when he did, Josephine took to her bed. He never returned. Then, one day, as she read a newspaper, something in it caused her to turn pale and she fainted. Her mother took up the paper, and after reading it, began to scream.

Peter figured that the young man had been killed, and not just him, but the father, too. Whatever did truly happen or was in the paper, he never heard of them again.

The next day, the mother called all the servants into Josephine's room. The young woman lay in bed, smiling and out of her head. They could tell she was dying. Just before she passed away, she said, "Tell Henri I'll always be waiting for him at the window," and with one long breath, she died.

Bryce was told by the old man that they shipped her body away for burial. Her mother and the servants packed up and left within a few days after. For a long time after that, the house stood deserted, the only sounds heard either the creaking of shutters or slamming of doors as the wind swept through its empty halls.

Over the years, it got the reputation of being haunted, for others, like Dr. Bryce, reported seeing a wraith-like face of a beautiful young woman at the window.

There were never any explanations found of who these people were or what happened to them; only that within those walls, dramas of love and sorrow, mystery and death had played out. All are now buried with those people long gone; the only evidence of it being the spirit of a girl still waiting for her lover to come for her.

Hawes House

A story told in *Virginia Ghosts*, by the author of the *Lassie* books, retold by L. B. Taylor in his *Ghosts of Richmond* and from others over the years, is the one involving the Hawes House in Richmond.

Mrs. Edward Terhune (whose pen name was Marion Harland) wrote about the ghost in a chapter of her autobiography, *The Story of My Life*. Her maiden name had been Mary Virginia Hawes, and she called the ghost everything from heroine to "Little Grey Lady" and even "Tortoise Shell Ghost."

From 1840 to 1875, the Hawes place was located at 506 East Leigh Street. A Colonial house built in the nineteenth century, it eventually gave way to the encroaching city. Back in 1840, when Virginia first encountered the ghost that winter night, things hadn't gotten to that point.

After seeing off a male visitor, Virginia locked the door and said good night to her parents in their room. She proceeded across the passageway that divided the two first-floor bedrooms. A small woman dressed in gray glided along the wall in front of her, disappearing at the Venetian blinds at the end of the front hall. Virginia noticed that her head bowed in her hands and that a high, carved tortoise shell comb decorated her hair.

Later when she wrote about it, she said, "I have reviewed the moment and its incident a thousand times to persuade myself that the apparition was an optical illusion or a trick of fancy. The 1,001st attempt results as did the first. I shut my eyes to see—always the one figure, the same motion, the same disappearance. She was dressed in gray; she was small and lithe; her head bowed upon her hands, and she slipped away, hugging the wall as if in flight, vanishing at the closed door. The door I heard myself latch itself five minutes ago! It did not open to let her through."

Frightened, Virginia rushed back to her parents' room, alerting them. Her father comforted her, and then walked her back to her room, telling her to try and sleep. The next day, he mentioned to her to keep her experience to herself, which she thought odd at the time.

A month later, in the evening, as she conversed with her father in the drawing room, her mother entered, saying that she had seen the ghost. She had noticed something white, like a turban, wrapped around the head. It shocked Virginia's father, but again, he asked that they keep it to themselves, which they did. Unfortunately, the manifestations continued. Virginia's young daughter, Mea, claimed something chased her down the stairs, and though she never saw it, insisted it wore high heels that tapped loudly on the steps. Once again, Mr. Hawes asked them not to talk of it.

Alice Hawes, Virginia's fourteen-year-old sister, along with a visiting cousin, had the next experience. Though sent to bed at nine, the girls slipped out to the parlor to talk for about an hour. When they decided to finally go back to bed, they found the hall dark, as the lamp had burned out. Moonlight poured through the window on the lower staircase, lighting the steps to the upper landing. They saw the white figure moving down the stairs. It appeared to be wearing a trailing white nightgown or nightshirt, with something white cast over its head. They thought it was one of the boys who had snuck down for a drink of water or a snack. Just then, the front door opened and all the boys in the house walked in, coming back from a nighttime stroll. The mysterious figure vanished right before their eyes. Both girls screamed, arousing everyone in the house.

Mr. Hawes called everyone together the next day. He admitted that it had proven useless to deceive themselves about the ghostly occurrences. He had known about them for a year or more; in fact, they hadn't been in the house more than three months when he became aware of the mystery.

It was after Mr. Hawes passed away, and the marriage of the sons and daughters, that Mrs. Hawes sold the house to the St. Paul's Episcopal Church. It was while workers were modifying it that the skeletal remains of a small woman were unearthed in the front of the premises. And yes, she had a tortoise shell comb beneath her skull! Speculation was that she'd been a murder victim.

Hollywood Cemetery

Hollywood Cemetery is a lovely place, a historical landmark still selected by individuals and families to provide a memorial for lost loved ones. Off to the right, just as you enter the cemetery through the Cherry Street entrance, is a very eerie-looking house, reminiscent of all the haunted house movies ever seen—and a chill runs up the spine. The caretaker's place. It brings home the fact that this is a place where the dead lie, and not a park where one can picnic and enjoy the view of the James River. Though in times past, families did visit the graves of loved ones and actually picnic there! People still visit it, though not to picnic, of course. Open from eight am to five pm daily the year round, and until six pm during Daylight Saving Time, it is a lovely, scenic place with loads of history behind it where one can still purchase a gravesite.

Founded in 1847, Hollywood Cemetery began as a delegation of Richmonders who drew plans after viewing other well-know burial sites in the country and making it in the "rural" style to escape the grid-lock monotony of older cemeteries. Paths wind through valleys, over hills, and beneath stately trees with natural tranquility, as if unplanned. The first gravesite sold was in 1849, though there are those residing there born as early as 1700. Some came from other cemeteries that had fallen prey to urban development. Many are buried there, including all nationalities, races, and religions—Major William Mayo, philanthropist James Thomas, Jr., Gustavus Myer, and Governor William A. Smith to 18,000 enlisted Confederate soldiers, and countless many more rest at peace in this cemetery.

Recognizing the place's appeal, they made sure early on to have some famous people buried there—people like the fifth president of the United States, James Monroe. Brought down from New York, he was interred at Hollywood instead of at his ancestral home at Sherwood Forest. The United States' tenth president, John Tyler, also lies there. President from 1841-1845, he opposed secession by the South before the Civil War broke out. He passed away in 1862, while serving in the Confederate Congress. Neither president, though, causes any of the ghostly happenings in the cemetery.

The first statesman to be buried there was John Randolph. He loved freedom and freed his slaves, but as an aristocrat, he hated the idea of equality and detested Thomas Jefferson. It is said that his soul must be so disturbed by American politics that by placing a hand on his gravestone, one can feel him trembling and turning in his grave. Others though, noticed that his trembling only happens whenever a coal train passes beneath the hill on which he rests.

Since Richmond was the capitol of the South during its succession and the Civil War, the president of the Confederate States, Jefferson Davis, was transferred from New Orleans to be buried at Hollywood Cemetery. As the body was transported by train, thousands of admirers in the Southern states littered the tracks with magnolia petals.

Confederate Granite Pyramid.

He was buried near his young son, Joe Davis, and his daughter, "Winnie." Joe's gravestone was purchased for forty dollars by the little boys and girls of the Southern capitol. As for Winnie, it is said that she died of a broken heart longing for her forbidden, abolitionist suitor. Near Davis is the Confederate general, J. E. B. Stuart.

Though they say that you won't find ghosts in cemeteries, there are ghostly legends abounding in this one. One is about the ninety-foot granite pyramid, built as a monument to the 18,000 enlisted Confederate soldiers buried near it. Unknown are 11,000—many of them brought in from Gettysburg, and interred enmasse in Hollywood. There have been those who swore they've heard soft moans from these graves on nights when the moon is full. Maybe these restless spirits call out, wanting only to go home.

Another story involves the statue of a cast iron dog. It stands almost in the shadow of the pyramid, and came originally from the front of a store on Broad Street in the nineteenth century. A little girl would always come by and pet it, talking to it and showing her love for it as if it were a real dog. But one day, she didn't come—and never did again. She had perished in an epidemic in 1892, and was buried in Hollywood Cemetery. Because of her affection for the cast-iron dog, though, it was placed at her grave site. Eerily, it stands there to this very day, as if guarding her. There have been those who say that it moves occasionally, that they would pass it pointing in one direction and come back, to find it staring the opposite way.

Not far away lies the tomb of famous author, Ellen Glasgow. After she passed away, it was discovered in her will a stipulation that her two pet dogs that preceded her in death be dug up from the backyard of her home and buried with her. There are those who claim to hear these two dogs running around and whining at the gravesite, late at night. Could Ellen be tossing them sticks to fetch?

Metal Dog by Child's Graveside.

Another story, creepy in the telling, is not a ghost story. It concerns the vampire supposedly buried in Hollywood. His name is W.W. Poole, and there are stories that the lock to the gate of his crypt is sometimes found opened, maybe even by "vampire hunters" wanting to stake him. Some say he was called a vampire due to a rare blood disease he had. An accountant in life, he passed away in the early 1920s. The crypt is only marked W.W. Poole, with no birth date, just the year of his death—1922. Supposedly, his remains had been stolen from the grave by Satanists and then found. Finally, his remains, and those of his wife, were removed to an another tomb in an undisclosed location to discourage further grave robbing attempts. The door to the original tomb was also welded shut.

Another take on this story—more urban legend than anything—has the vampire being some strange creature that had dug its way out of the Church Hill train tunnel cave-in and was found over a victim, his mouth covered in blood. He had jagged teeth, plus decomposing skin hanging off his arms and legs. The creature took off and ran all the way to Hollywood Cemetery, followed by pursuers, where he hid in a crypt marked W. W. Poole.

This is obviously an urban legend, with a basis in fact. The creature was, in reality, a fireman, Benjamin F. Mosby, burned almost beyond recognition. He had been rushed to Grace Hospital, dying twenty-four hours later. An out of the ordinary offshoot from this was the saying that *going to Hollywood* meant you were dying.

Another interesting story is the tragic one involving Jefferson Davis, President of the Confederate States of America. His five-year-old son, Joe, had fallen to his death from a balcony at the White House of the Confederacy. There are stories of a little boy seen near the former White House, wandering the streets and then disappearing.

In 1913, when Jefferson's body was exhumed from its burial spot in New Orleans and brought back to Richmond to be reinterred at Hollywood Cemetery, he was reburied so that the grave of his son was at his feet. With all that happened to him—his son's death, the Civil War, and being uprooted to be reburied—one would think he would haunt, but apparently not. Instead, it seems that he has found peace after death.

A wonderful location of both beauty and history, this is a place to come and enjoy, ghosts not withstanding. And who knows? Maybe you might see more than great architecture or lovely scenery. It's a cemetery, after all.

W. W. Poole's "The Richmond Vampire" Crypt.

Parker's Battery Richmond National Battlefield Park in Chester, Virginia.

The Assorted Civil War Ghosts of Richmond

Parapsychologists claim that those who are killed suddenly, in tragic or traumatic circumstances, can cause hauntings to occur. And because the State of Virginia held the bloodiest and most bitter section of the South during this conflict in our nation's history, it stands to reason that it would have more Civil War ghosts then anywhere else. Richmond contributes its own share of Civil War spirits to that state number.

One such place is Cold Harbor, a historical battlefield park in Mechanicsville, where 7,000 Union soldiers fell in less than half an hour. Apparently, battles are still going on there, usually at one o'clock in the morning, according to those hearing the sounds.

In Chester, there's a battery off Ware Springs Bottom Road. Now a Richmond National Battlefield Park site, it was part of the Confederate defense line that trapped Butler in 1864-65. Observers claimed to have heard voices coming from the Civil War bunkers there, even when there was no one alive there.

At the Battery 9 station in Petersburg, observers remarked that they have heard loud noises and sounds of cannons going off, mainly late at night. A ghostly figure on a black horse has also been seen, just at the top of the hill behind the station.

In Hopewell, there's Appomattox Manor, an old house on the river front known to be a last holdout for Confederate, and even Union, soldiers. One legend that surrounds the house is told about a nurse who hid a Union soldier in the wall of the basement when Confederate soldiers came to inspect the house. On finding Union paraphernalia in the storage room, they arrested her and took her away. But the Union soldier, unable to escape, died. Sounds of scratching at the walls can still be heard. Obviously the soldier still wants to be let out of his hiding place, even over a hundred years later.

In Varina, Battlefield Cemetery has a ghost that has been lurking around. If someone drinks from the water fountain in the yard, the ghost makes noises and throws things at the person. He is believed to be a Confederate soldier.

Another ghostly legend centers on a planned siege of Richmond in early 1864. There's everything that makes a good ghost story, from a young black hung to a mutilation of the Raid's leader. Something that Shakespeare or even Poe might have made up, except it really happened.

At that time, Richmonders had fears not only of the city being sacked and set fire to, but of rumors circulating that Jefferson Davis and his entire cabinet were to be executed. With thoughts of retaliation in their minds, it was murmured that maybe the 15,000 Union prisoners at Belle Isle should be hung. Luckily, others quelled those ideas.

An ingenious plan hatched by Brigadier General Judson Kilpatrick of the Union Army didn't work and the Capitol of the Confederacy didn't fall. But still, it led to what is now known as Dahlgren's Raid.

With Lee's Army of Northern Virginia fighting in the wilderness somewhere else, it was thought that this would be the perfect time to attack Richmond, being vulnerable as it was. Kilpatrick convinced that leading a detachment of 4,000 Union soldiers through Southern lines into the city would be easy. He would draw attention, thus enabling a smaller troop of 500 men to sneak in and cross the James River to set the Union prisoners free. It would definitely break the Confederate spirit, be daring, and also successful in the bargain.

To lead the smaller raiding party, a soldier named Ulric Dahlgren was chosen. The youngest colonel in the Northern Army at the age of twenty-one, he'd gotten wounded in an earlier skirmish at Boonsboro, Maryland, and had had his right leg amputated. But months later, and fitted with a wooden leg, he eagerly took the command.

The plan had all the elements for failure, from bad weather to confusion and Confederate snipers picking them off with accuracy. Things grew worse. Even when a young black told Dahlgren he could lead them across the river safely, he led them instead to a treacherous place, swollen by storms. Dahlgren thought the man had betrayed him and had him hung.

The whole mission lost, Dahlgren ordered a retreat. Separated in the darkness, 300 of his men made it safely back to the Union lines, while Dahlgren and rest of his men became lost.

Dahlgren headed northeast. He crossed the Mattaponi River and treaded through the wood, yelling, "Surrender, you damned Rebels, or I'll shoot you!" Shots rang out. Hit, he fell from his mount, dead. Most of his men either died or were captured. With no mercy, Dahlgren's body was attacked. A finger was cut off just to get a ring, while his artificial leg, his watch, and other valuables and papers were confiscated. Carted off in a lidless pine box to Richmond, his body was displayed in a railroad station. Later, after being interred, the body was dug back up to be buried again.

The papers that Dahlgren had on him about the purpose of the raid supposedly came to light, though they may have been false documents. The contents, placed in the press, mentioned that thousands of Union prisoners were to have been freed and this terrified the citizens of Richmond even more as they envisioned pictures of rape, murder, and even more being visited upon them. At the same time, Northern papers decried Dahlgren's brutalized body, the hanging of the black man, and the use of bloodhounds to track down the other Union soldiers. Lee sent a message to General Meade of the Union Army about the barbarous acts, and Meade replied that no orders had ever been given for any cities to be burned or civilians killed.

Two ghostly tales came out of this.

One told of an old house on Three Chopt Road where some of Dahlgren's men stopped, trying to discover where the household silver had been hidden. A slave there refused to tell where it had been buried and the men strung him up by his thumbs. There are claims that his spirit still haunts the place.

The other tale is about one of Dahlgren's young officers. He had ridden his horse into a honeysuckle thicket somewhere on Cary Street. An ice house had once stood there. He fell in and died. On calm nights there are those who say they can still hear his moans.

Reveille

Located on West Cary Street in Richmond's West End is a Federal-style country house, now used now as administrative offices for the Reveille United Methodist Church since it was bought in 1951.

A tall, white-painted brick house of simple eighteenth-century design, it has a large garden with box-bordered flower beds in the back. When built, Reveille was a plantation house far outside the city. Tradition attributes its title to the Revolutionary period, but the name is not found in deed books earlier than 1852. And yet, it is known from the diary of Miss Rebecca Williams that she and her family lived in it circa 1806. It is also said that many houses of the same type were built around 1790-1820. And many articles written have attributed this one to being older—one even stating that it is one of the oldest houses in Richmond, and "is viewed as more original in its structure than any other in the city except possibly the Poe Shrine." The same article mentions that it could have been erected as early as 1720 on a land grant from the King of England to the Kennons. Of course, the debate is on exactly when it was built.

Edgar Allan Poe was a guest there once, along with the naturist, Audubon, who was a frequent visitor when he stayed with his friend, General Richardson, across the road at Windsor. There are crosses carved on the paneled doors, done to keep the witches away. Apparently, it did keep the witches away, but not the ghosts.

An unusual feature is the secret chamber in the house, built as a hiding place from Indians—so secret that, for generations, many did not know it existed. It was discovered in the twentieth century when boxes were stored into the garret below it. The only way it can be reached is through a hole in the attic. One has to climb a ladder to a trapdoor and crawl through the narrow hole cut in a hand-sewn beam that runs the length of the house. The chamber is five-by-ten feet long and eight feet deep, with no doors or windows.

Reveille has seen tragic deaths. Elizabeth Crutchfield Blair, last descendent and heiress of the house, died in 1849. Before that, the family chauffeur shot and killed her husband. Another tragic death happened to one of the Kennons' daughters. One night, she ran down the steep flight of stone steps to her lover, who waited outside with two horses so they could elope. Halfway down, she tripped and fell headlong to her death. They claim that her grave could be seen in the back of the garden, earlier in the twentieth century.

Hers is one of the specters. On moonlit nights, riderless horses are heard, galloping around the house. It is also said that she glides through the trapdoor, to go through the attic and down the winding stairs to the second floor. There, she pauses. Claims of the swish of a skirt, too soft to be a rustle, can be heard outside the door of the front room to the right of the hall. It is considered the haunted room.

Someone who once was a guest at Reveille was awakened at midnight, by the knob of the door to her room turning. Someone entered the room, crossed the floor to the mahogany wardrobe and rummaged through it. The guest switched on the light and the mysterious interloper vanished.

One servant refused to sleep in the house, not wanting to "encounter the haunt." And during the nineteenth century, people avoided the house when walking because of its reputation of being haunted. White shapes could be seen flitting past the windows, and even a report that "many see a British soldier hanging from a tree." And in Karen McLeod's report, instead of the riding habit that the girl who fell to her death wore, it's a wedding gown, which can better explain the swishing sounds.

In the *Richmond Times Dispatch,* earlier in the twentieth century, in its Sunday section, is the declaration that "a veritable colony of ghosts reside at that loveliest of Tuckahoe homes, Reveille." In that article, it was written that a company of ghosts is heard but never seen in one of the bedrooms. It is also states that they don't terrorize anyone, as they seem oblivious to all but their own interests.

It goes on to mention that one spirit beats a frantic tattoo on the doors of the old wardrobe it's imprisoned in, while on the stairs the rustle of starched skirts against the rails can be heard. There's also an old lady, dressed in a long cape and bonnet. She never leaves the basement dining room. She keeps herself busy with papers in a closet, not paying any attention to those around her, just self-absorbed in her own affairs.

Elizabeth Crutchfield Blair passed away in 1949, leaving a will that bequeathed it to the Association for the Preservation of Virginia Antiquities. The Association voted not to accept it, as they felt it would have been too expensive to maintain, especially as Mrs. Blair stated that the grounds and house were not to be changed.

In 1951, the Reveille United Methodist Church bought it, and it is still owned by them. The pastor of the church, Dr. Hasbrouck Hughes, and his staff are aware of the ghostly stories and admitted to joking about it a lot. But as far as he knew, no one has admitted to experiencing anything supernatural, neither by sight or hearing.

No doubt the ghosts felt that Reveille is in capable, spiritual hands and have departed for good.

Scotchtown

For seven years in the 1700s, the great Virginia orator and statesman, Patrick Henry, lived at Scotchtown, a huge sprawling estate in upper Hanover County, a few miles west of Ashland off Route 54. Believed to have been built in 1719, Scotchtown is, says the Virginia Landmarks Register, "probably the largest one-story colonial house in the commonwealth."

On July 15, 1717, Charles Chiswell received a grant of 9,976 acres of new land in Hanover County from Lieutenant Governor Alexander Spotswood, "in consideration of the sum of fifty pounds of good and lawfull mony." He built the house known today as Scotchtown. The construction of the house is dated 1719, based on the supposition that land grantees were required to build within two years of receiving a grant. If any structure was on the present Scotchtown site in 1719, it was most definitely smaller than what is there today. Chiswell's initial dwelling may well have been elsewhere on his property. But a date range of roughly the second quarter of the eighteenth century seems the most reasonable for the present structure.

Whenever it truly happened, Chiswell and his wife, Esther, soon moved to their new property. Besides the agricultural production, Chiswell also established an iron manufactory nearby. William Byrd described his 1732 visit to Chiswell's iron manufactory in his "Progress to the Mines," in which he describes Chiswell as "a sensible, well bred man and very frank in communicating his knowledge in the mystery of making iron, wherein he has had long experience." He described the house as "very clean and [everything] very good," although apparently the house was fairly small because Byrd lodged elsewhere.

Charles Chiswell passed away in 1737. The property was inherited by his son, Colonel John Chiswell, who moved his family, which grew to include four daughters, to the property. They remained there until 1752 or 1753, and then relocated to Williamsburg.

Archaeological evidence suggests that the house was expanded to its present size during this period. It also obtained its present name during Colonel Chiswell's occupancy. The 1757 sale of property by Colonel Chiswell first gives the name "Scotch Town" for the house on his Hanover property.

In 1759 or 1760, Colonel Chiswell's son-in-law, John Robinson, took ownership of Scotchtown, most likely as partial payment for debts. Robinson does not appear to have ever lived at the property. In 1766, Colonel Chiswell murdered a man at Mosby's Tavern, died while on bail, and was refused burial in Williamsburg. His body was returned to Scotchtown. The same year, Robinson himself died, deeply indebted to the state. In order to repay some of Robinson's debts, Scotchtown was offered for sale, eventually selling in 1770, to an unnamed buyer.

Patrick Henry, his wife Sarah, and their six children are the first known inhabitants of Scotchtown after the Chiswells moved out. Patrick Henry and his family probably took occupancy in the spring of 1771, because by September, he was producing tobacco there, which he sold to a local store owner. At about that time, Sarah Henry began showing signs of mental illness. Eventually, she had to be confined, probably in a small basement apartment. She died at Scotchtown in 1775.

During his years at Scotchtown, Henry became busy with civic activities. It was from Scotchtown that he rode in 1775, to St. John's Church in Richmond, where he delivered his famous "Liberty or Death" speech. He rode from there again in 1776 to be elected first governor of Virginia. In 1777, Henry married his second wife, Dorothea Dandridge, and relocated to the Governor's Palace in Williamsburg. Scotchtown was offered for sale that year and again in 1778. Little is known about the house during Henry's time there. Few domestic accounts from this period, clouded as it was by family sorrow and political upheaval, survive.

It was apparent though that Henry wasn't happy at Scotchtown, due to Sarah's mental illness. She was confined—no one knows how long—to two rooms in the cold, damp basement of the house, rarely seen by anyone. When Sarah finally died, she was buried in an unmarked grave, then the custom for the interment of "crazy" people.

It went through numerous owners for 180 years and eventually was abandoned. For a time, it was occupied by squatters who kept goats in the basement and raised chickens in one of the first-floor rooms. In 1958, the Association for the Preservation of Virginia Antiquities bought Scotchtown and restored it to its former dignity and integrity.

But the Association soon learned that Scotchtown was haunted. Multiple spirits have been seen or heard here, but the predominant one is Sarah Henry. Ron Steele, Scotchtown's director, declares that if it wasn't haunted, it should be! As he says, "It is a very spooky place, especially at night when the wind is blowing. It can get very scary inside. You hear all kinds of noises."

Steele and his wife, Alice, keep check on the house during the off season. There are occasions when both Steele and the local police feel reluctant to go into the house at night. There are motion alarm systems inside, and always they are set off. Steele says that someone or something has to be at least four feet tall to set them off. In the past few years, the alarms have been set off a number of times, and when the police come, they ask Steele to enter first.

One of the most frightening phenomena has to do with the portrait of Joseph Shelton that hangs in the dining room. It has been said that you can enter at night and feel certain that the portrait's eyes follow you all across the room, no matter where you go.

Pieces of furniture also seem to get moved around inexplicably at times, and the sound of chains being dragged across the floor of the attic can be heard when no one is up there.

Several years ago, a tour guide took some tourists through the house. The group stopped in the dining room, which was directly above the room occupied by Sarah in the basement. When the guide started to tell the story of Sarah, suddenly the group heard shrill screams emanating from the basement. Everyone left the house as fast as they could.

Mary Adams, who resides nearby, lived at Scotchtown from 1933 to 1940, and experienced all sorts of strange phenomena, like a lot of unnatural sounds—chains dragging across the floor and other weird noises. Once, as she was playing in the house with other children, they all saw a figure in a long flowing gown, all in white. The children knew it wasn't a real person. They watched it for a half minute or more, and then it disappeared. They bolted out of there. Even after Mary moved, she would always get the feeling, whenever she visited, that the ghost lady was there. Did she ever think it was Sarah Henry? She couldn't be sure, but it could have been.

Berkeley Plantation

At Harrison's Landing on the James River on scenic Route 5, between Richmond and Williamsburg, lies Berkeley Plantation. This historic location claims to have hosted the first official Thanksgiving in 1619, beating out Plymouth Rock. Part of a grant made in 1619 by King James I to the Berkeley Company, it was designated "Berkeley Hundred." On Good Friday in 1622, a band of Indians stormed the settlement and killed nine people. Years later, it was abandoned and not reclaimed until 1636. Eventually, it became the property of John Bland, a merchant from London. His son, Giles Bland was a favored lieutenant of Nathaniel Bacon, a rebellion leader of Bacon's Rebellion. When Bacon's insurrection failed in 1676, Giles was ordered to be hanged by Governor Sir William Berkeley. Berkeley came into possession by Benjamin Harrison III and it was his son, Benjamin Harrison IV, who built the original Georgian mansion in 1726, out of brick fired on the plantation.

The birthplace of William Henry Harrison, the ninth president of the United States, and Benjamin Harrison V, signer of the Declaration of Independence, Berkeley Plantation is also the ancestral home of Benjamin Harrison, our twenty-third president. The mansion occupies a beautifully landscaped hilltop site that overlooks the historic James River. The date of the building and the initials of the owners, Benjamin Harrison IV and his wife, Anne, appear in a date stone over a side door. The mansion is said to be the oldest three-story brick house in Virginia that can prove its date, and the first with a pediment roof. The Adam woodwork and the double arches of the 'Great Rooms' in the mansion were installed by Benjamin Harrison VI in 1790 at the direction of Thomas Jefferson.

Five terraced gardens lead from the house to the James River, dug by hand before the Revolutionary War. Flowers bloom, spring through autumn, and there are many hundred-year old trees in the restored boxwood garden, offering breathtaking vistas of the James River. On the adjacent farmland, sheep graze in the distant rolling hills along the river on this almost 1,000-acre plantation where miles of old-fashioned gravel roads forge through it. Wildlife abounds in this delightful, peaceful setting. A small woodland glade nestles in the trees beside an expansive glimpse of the James River and rolling fields. Anyone can linger at the river's edge, enjoying the gentle lapping water and soft river breezes, while taking a tour of the plantation, open daily from nine am to five pm. It's only closed on Thanksgiving and Christmas. To find out more: check the website at http://www.berkeley-plantation.com/.

Surely, such a place can't be haunted?

But, yes, it is.

One dark and stormy night in 1744, Benjamin Harrison IV dashed through the mansion, closing windows and locking shutters. One upstairs window gave him particular trouble and he called for help. Two of his daughters, one carrying Benjamin's infant son, Benjamin Harrison V, came to help. Just then, a flash of lightening struck them and all were killed except the baby. A doctor happened to be a dinner guest at the mansion at the time. He "bled" young Benjamin, who survived and grew up to become President of the American Colonies, sign the Declaration of Independence, and marry, and sired William Henry Harrison, an Indian fighter. William, or "Tippecanoe," as he was nicknamed, was elected to become the ninth president of the U. S., while his grandson, Benjamin Harrison, became the twenty-third.

It is said that Benjamin Harrison IV and at least one of the daughters never left Berkeley and are the specters haunting it. Many of the residents, staff members, and even visitors over the years have had encounters.

One of the common manifestations has to do with the balky bedroom window. Periodically, it slams shut by itself.

Others tell of seeing a young woman with a baby in her arms, standing at the window late at night, but when investigated nothing is found.

There's also a legend of a ghost in the bottom, a dip in the road that leads to the mansion and is believed to be haunted by a young child who cries at night. It has been discounted by some to be only an owl. It is believed that plantation owners encouraged the tale to keep slaves in their quarters at night. The owners felt this kept the slaves fresh for working in the morning and thought the ghost tale did more good than harm.

A photographer who visited the plantation took still pictures; one of the portrait of Mrs. Jamieson's great grandmother, Elizabeth Burford, in the south parlor. After he developed the film, he found a picture of another person entirely. He thought that the staff moved the portraits—no one had. He rented a television camera and set it up in the house to shoot for a proposed documentary. But when he did, the camera wouldn't work. When he took it back to the camera shop, it worked with no problem.

A tour guide, Vickey Hoover, had a number of things happen to her, and she feels it's the spirit of Benjamin Harrison. Not a believer when she joined the staff, she became one quickly.

Vickey said that, most likely, Benjamin thought she was being disrespect-ful. She had been standing in the front hall beside the linen press, when the door swung open and smacked her on the shoulder. It happened to her three or four more times after that. Explaining the phenomenon to some tourists one time, the door swung open, and she had to show them that she hadn't pressed any secret lever to make it open. Another time, she had returned from maternity leave and joked that Benjamin must not know she was back. Suddenly, she heard three knocks, and she turned and watched as the door swung open.

Both she and another tour guide would hear rattling from time to time. She was in the laundry alone one day and heard the rattling of a door. The cry of a baby could be heard, too, in the basement, but when she checked she found nothing. When she went back upstairs to the breakfast room, the crying halted altogether.

Another weird phenomenon occurs whenever anyone walks across the floor in the front parlor. When someone passes the candelabra, glass tinkles in it.

Another time, Mrs. Jamieson called over to the tour guides in the adjacent building from the main house, demanding to know who was in her attic. She was adamant about the footsteps she heard from up there. One of the guides checked out the attic, but found the door bolted shut as it always was. She even went outside to see if any workmen had a ladder propped up against the building and were working around the attic, but again, nothing.

The Berkeley dining room is where most of the manifestations occur. Many tourists claim to feel a presence the minute they walk into the dining room. Most of it centers around a fruit bowl on the dining room table. One of the tour guides, Virginia Anders, put an apple in the bowl and before she even left the room, heard it drop. Turning around, she saw the apple sail through the air and go over a Chinese screen. Frightened, she bolted from the room as fast as she could. Others have seen apples come out and fall to the floor. One time, a lemon, fixed to a nail in the bowl, popped out and rolled across the table on its own. Most of the fruit phenomena happen in the winter time, around January, February, and March.

Once, just before the first tour of the morning, peanuts were discovered scattered across the table. The guide, Jan Wycoff, who discovered them, asked Vickey Hoover about them, wondering where they had come from. She told Vickery to clean it up when she came through, but later, Hoover told her she never saw any peanuts in the room. They had vanished.

Whatever the reason for the fruit bowl phenomena, no one has an answer. Maybe Benjamin Harrison just doesn't like the arrangement. Who knows?

Berkeley.

Ghosts Haunt
More than Houses

Specters haunt more than just houses. They can haunt aviation museums, schools, and more.

The Virginia Aviation Museum

The Virginia Aviation Museum is located near the Richmond Airport and contains old planes and aviation artifacts beginning in World War II to present day, on what once was a Civil War battlefield. Ghostly occurrences have happened there. Like footsteps that lead up to a particular plane in the museum, and a very old stopwatch that starts up and begins to tick.

Manchester Rescue Squad

Another haunting happened many years ago in the former Manchester Rescue Squad headquarters in Henrico County. At that time, the building was already thirty years old. But no doubt, the haunting began long before the place had been built.

Whatever the reason, squad members experienced persistent hauntings. Nothing had been ever seen, only heard, and usually after the crew on duty went to bed. Sounds like the front door opening and closing, with footsteps going through the doorway could be heard. Next, those same footsteps headed to the bay area where the emergency vehicles were kept and the doors on the units could be heard opening and closing. When someone would get up to investigate, they found nothing. Explanations arose that maybe the building was settling, or even that the furnace was the cause. But this logic never helped in the spring, when neither the furnace nor the air conditioner was in use.

One of the squad members, Harry Boyd, said that, one night, it sounded like all the dishes in the kitchen shattered and the silverware dumped. When everyone went to discover what happened, nothing seemed out of place. Once, a rookie dared the spirit to reveal itself. Later that night, sounds like someone striking at the walls with a sledgehammer and caving the walls in filled the air. Not gentle taps, but thunder-booming sounds, coming from both the ceiling and the men's bunk room. It began at about eleven pm and finally halted at five the next morning.

At one point, the sounds were recorded. Twenty minutes of rapping filled one tape. Another tape had sounds like someone clinking glasses together.

As the visitations became regular, the crew decided to name the ghost Clarence. Now, "Clarence" never did anything violent, just made a lot of noise. Some volunteers quit out of fear, and things got so bad that many refused to sit by themselves at night.

One crew member offered up a possible explanation. With many dying in the back of the ambulances, it seemed reasonable to expect spirits to be left over. Dr. Glenn Hawkes, a psychologist and parapsychology instructor at Virginia Commonwealth University at that time, agreed with this theory. His opinion is that any place where strong emotional or violent events happened often does have some kind of effect that persists over long periods of time, until that place is torn down or removed. Eventually, the squad moved on to a new location. Nothing has been reported there out of the ordinary.

Matoaca Middle School

Schools can be haunted, too. One of these schools is in Matoaca, part of Chesterfield County. Formerly Matoaca High School, it became Matoaca Middle School when a new high school was built. When it was still the high school, it was thought that the theatre was haunted. Lights would be seen moving and turning off by themselves, doors would shake, and something kept banging on the door. Other noises had been heard too, along with a cold chill felt by some.

First Antioch Baptist Church and
Fire Creek Baptist Church Graveyards

Off 522, a road that winds from Midlothian to Powhatan, there's First Antioch Baptist Church, with a graveyard in the back. Susan Swartz loved to take her camera to different graveyards and take photographs. In many of her pictures, faces and orbs appear—there and at the one at Fire Creek Baptist Church on Route 711. Susan said that at the First Antioch graveyard, though, she developed an overwhelming urge to get out. Just then, someone or something pushed her out of the place. She hasn't been back since.

An African-American Haunt

Another story about a cemetery happened to Rachel, who works for the Chesterfield Historical Society's Central Committee on preserving graveyards. She had been at an African-American cemetery in Powhatan County, copying gravestones. Suddenly, a voice came into her head, more like a thought than an actual voice, saying, "Hey, what about us?" She looked over the cemetery, finding no one, so resumed copying gravestones onto her list. Once again, the same voice came into her head, "Hey, what about us?" So she went carefully down each row, looking for what the voice asked. Finally she saw a kind of fluffy bush and underneath were two funeral home markers with the names and dates of both births and deaths on them. Two brothers had passed away as old men in the 1980s. She copied down their information and hasn't been back there since.

Haunted Shopping Centers

New homes and shopping centers are popping up all over Richmond. Sometimes, the land the buildings are being built upon are just empty lots. Other times there's another building on the acreage or a family cemetery plot. One such place was the Johnson family plot, near the intersection of Huguenot Road and Alverser Drive. The graveyard was removed and a shopping center that included a Barnes and Noble bookstore were built there. Stores occupying the buildings opposite Barnes and Nobles, and even Barnes and Noble itself, have had many strange things happen there after all had been opened for business years ago. Currently, a worker at Barnes and Noble says she has never seen or heard anything. I've not felt or seen anything there, either. But maybe, as you explore the ghostly stories of Richmond upon their shelves, you might feel a strange presence ...

Castlewood

Also reported by Pattie Grady, who is with Chesterfield Historical Society's Cemetery Committee, she says that she has heard that Parke Poindexter haunts Castlewood that houses the library and offices of the Historical Society. He was the house's builder, and if you go there, you can see his portrait that still hangs there.

The Ghosts of Bellgrade—Ruth's Chris Steak House

Ruth's Chris Steak House is an upscale restaurant at 11500 Huguenot Road in Midlothian, where the servers wear tuxedos and the food is scrumptious. But, besides great, expensive food, this place has spirits.

Way before it was ever a place to dine, it had been a one and one half story farmhouse, built in 1732. Several families had lived in it from its construction until 1824, when one Edward Friend purchased it from Edward Cox.

During the time the Friend family occupied it, the family grew both in size and wealth, and the farm grew to approximately one thousand acres. To accommodate the growing family, the house was remodeled. The wings were added, the front door and fireplace moved, and a front porch and columns added on. It became known as the Bellgrade Plantation.

In 1840, the Friends sold the place to a forty-three-year old French bachelor named Robiou. Robiou met the fourteen-year-old daughter of a prominent attorney and wealthy landowner named Wormley, who lived on Old Gun Road. He asked for, and got, her hand in marriage, marrying not long after. The couple moved into Bellgrade.

After only a few weeks of marriage, Robiou arrived home one afternoon and discovered his young wife in a compromising situation with her previous nineteen-year-old boyfriend, Reid. Angry, he threw her out of the house and demanded a divorce.

Incensed, her father convinced her lover to help him retaliate against Robiou. They waited for Robiou to return home late one evening, and when he reached his porch, Wormley fatally shot him. Both Wormley and Reid were arrested and taken to Chesterfield Courthouse to be put in jail.

Reid was released, as he had been duped into the plot by the older and more cunning man, plus he had not pulled the trigger. Wormley was tried for murder, but because he had many acquaintances in the judicial system, he convinced the clerk of the court into giving whiskey to several members of the jury, in hopes of getting a mistrial. He got the mistrial, but the case obtained so much notoriety that the judge went ahead and retried him. This time he was found guilty and sentenced to hang.

Wormley tried to appeal his conviction, while the daughter, now a widow and neither divorced nor disinherited, married her young lover and moved back into the plantation. Failing the appeal, Wormley was hanged before a crowd of six thousand people, the largest at that time ever to witness a hanging in Virginia.

Within two weeks of the execution, Robiou's widow fell down the front stairs of the plantation home and died. There are two accounts of how she died. One says she fell on a sewing basket and a pair of scissors punctured her heart, while the other story claims that she broke her neck. Whichever one is true, since her death; there have been hundreds of stories of sightings of the ghosts of both Robiou and his unfaithful wife roaming the boxwood gardens behind the home.

Another interesting story about this place comes from the time of the Civil War. During that time, Bellgrade was used both by General A. P. Hill, as his headquarters while he engaged in a campaign between Richmond and Petersburg, and also as a hospital for Southern soldiers. Hill died during this campaign. They tried to take his body to Hollywood Cemetery, but couldn't get it across the James River due to the damage to the bridge and the presence of Union troops. Instead, he was taken to Bellgrade and buried in the Friend family cemetery. In his last will and testament, Hill requested to be buried standing up at Bellgrade. When the war ended and Hill was moved to Hollywood Cemetery, once again, he was buried standing up. And when a statue in his honor was created and his body was moved for the last time, they buried him under the statue standing up.

Later, residents of the plantation changed the name of the place to Belvedere and, even later on, to Alandale. The last people to live in the old home were the Hoppers.

In the early 1990s, the property came into Clay Thomasson's hands. He opened Ruth's Chris Steak House in the house. Only a few have had experiences with the ghosts. John Romano, a manager at Ruth's Chris had arrived for a special event early one morning, half asleep. The lights outside were dim and yet, when he peered out of the three bay windows toward the patio he saw something that looked like a hot road when the heat warps the air.

A former employee of Ruth's Chris Steak House told of a time when a mirror shattered; a strange incident as no one had been near it. The cook, at that time, had come out and said that he always wondered if the place was haunted, as one time, four or five pots and pans of his had fallen down for no reason whatsoever.

When you enter the restaurant, in the living room, off behind the desk where the hostess stands, you'll find Friend family memorabilia donated by John Friend, great grandson of Dr. Edward Friend. John Friend passed away in 1995. A biographical history of the Friend family, done by John, is available for viewing on the desk in the living room.

Front of Ruth's Chris Steak House at night.

Crab Louie's Seafood Tavern

There's a very good seafood restaurant in the town of Midlothian. Besides having great food and being of historical interest, it is also haunted.

Once called Midlothian, the house, circa 1745, was owned by the wealthy Wooldridge family. Later, Abraham S. Wooldridge, who had a reputation for hospitality, used the house as a stop for the old Lynchburg-Richmond stagecoach.

In 1875, John J. Jewett bought the property and renamed it, "The Sycamores," after the sycamore trees that grew in the area. He and his wife had six children there and ran a boarding school. Later on, in the mid-1900s, his descendent used it for a nursery school. The Jewett family owned it for one hundred years.

In 1975, it was opened as The Sycamore Inn, a restaurant, with the surrounding acreage made into the Sycamore Square Village Shopping Center. A year later, a fire burned down the east wing and it was rebuilt. In 1981, it became Crab Louie's.

The owner, Floyd Sinkler, thought that they had several ghosts. In the summer of 1985, he sat at the bar one night after closing, and suddenly got the feeling that someone stood behind him. He turned around and found himself facing the upper half of a man dressed in clothing from the nineteenth century. What he saw looked like a black suit with a white collar. The man also had a powdery face. The man turned and vanished as he headed toward the attic.

Over the years, other occurrences happened. Once, a truck jumped the curb and knocked all the power lines out. Sinkler was doing some bookwork by hand when a loud crash came. It was a load of ice dumping in the ice machine, which was impossible since the power was out. Next, a roll of paper poured out of an electric adding machine—all by itself. He assumed the power had come back on. But a lineman told him that it hadn't.

On other occasions, people would run into the restaurant and claim that they saw flames shooting out of the chimney and thought the restaurant was on fire. Of course, there wasn't a fire.

Then there's the haunted table, Table 10. A group of ten to twelve people lingered late one night. Everyone but Sinkler and one waiter, Scott, had gone home. When the party finally left, Sinkler and Scott went to reset the table. After being told by his boss to go bring out some more bread plates, Scott said, "Floyd, we already brought them out." Sinkler remembered they had, but the plates had vanished.

Another time, as Sinkler, and this time, another server, stacked paper napkins for Table 10, the napkins fluttered off the table and landed in a single pile on the floor—all in sequence. They couldn't blame it on the breeze, either, as the window was closed and there was not even a hint of draft in the place.

Another time, Sinkler heard some children singing the happy birthday song from Table 10. He asked a waitress where the children were and she said, "That's not funny, Floyd." When he asked what she meant by that, she said she heard the singing, too, but that there had been no one at the table.

Two new employees learned about the hauntings right on their first day working, when three drawers on a bread warmer cabinet opened and slammed shut right in front of them.

But it was due to "Rachel," as the employees came to know, that the goings-on occurred. All of these particular happenings were during 1995-1996. Glasses flew off bar racks, landing several feet away. One glass even flew over a man's shoulder and struck another one on the foot. Both men sat about ten feet away from the bar racks, and numerous diners and employees witnessed this.

One night, a busboy and a couple of servers decided to use a Ouija board to find out who was causing the ruckus. The name Rachel spelled out, when they asked who was haunting their establishment. Rachel then told them she was a six or seven year old girl and was afraid to come out in the open; this was why no one ever saw her. The interesting thing about this was that when Sinkler told his daughter, Kelsey, about this, she thought that the ghost child was lonely and gave him one of her dolls to put in the restaurant. After he did as his daughter suggested, Rachel's glass-throwing ceased.

A chilling footnote to the Rachel incident happened in 1993. An airline pilot came into the tavern. He told Sinkler that he was a descendent of the Wooldridge family. Sinkler mentioned Rachel and the man went on to say that one of the first Wooldridge daughters who lived and died in the house at age six or seven had been named Rachel.

The Haunted Table 10 is on the left.

Today, Rachel still haunts Crab Louie's. One manager is gone, but manager Bruce Wilson, who's been there twenty years, has remained. He admits that though many things that have happened can be explained, there are still other phenomena that can't be so easily explained away. Like the glasses at the bar. He'd find some of the glasses on the floor where, minutes before, they'd been hung up. If they had fallen from that height, they should have been broken. Instead, they were not. He also mentioned the famous table, next to the fireplace, and that many people have seen the little girl standing by it.

Another time, late one night as he was closing up, a calculator started working, all by itself. He finally had to unplug it to make it stop. But there was no reason he could see why it would do this.

Next time you're in the mood for crab, call and reserve a table at Crab Louie's. If you're lucky, you might get the haunted table—even catch a glimpse of the ghost. And if not, the food is worth dining there. For the menu and more information, check out their website at http://www.crablouies.com/index.html.

Lady in Red at Wrexham Hall

Over the years, observers of ghostly phenomena have seen wraith-like forms of ladies, usually dressed in gray or white. Rarely has one been viewed in vivid colors, which makes the "Lady in Red" at Wrexham Hall in Chesterfield County an unusual spirit indeed.

Once, the house had been located on Route 10, until the land was sold, making way for the Chesterfield Meadows Shopping Center. Then it was taken apart and put up a couple streets behind the shopping center. Today it is on Wrexham Road.

Wrexham Hall is actually made up of two houses. One wing is older and from another house called Fruit Hill, an abandoned farm house on Swift Creek off Brander's Bridge Road. That place was built around 1750. Wrexham Hall's owners had been seeking suitable period flooring to replace flooring that had been deteriorating. The Fruit Hill owners wanted the whole house sold, and not just the flooring, and so that was how it became a part of Wrexham Hall.

Archibald Walthall, a captain of the Chesterfield Militia during the Revolutionary War, built Wrexham. Various sources give the date from 1700 to 1800, and even 1830.

Wrexham Hall.

As one report from the Virginia Historical Landmarks Commission states: "The fireplace mantels are the outstanding architectural gems in the house. The mantel in the dining room has open flutes and it has been indicated by someone that this dates the house prior to 1780."

When Walthall passed away, he left the house and property to his daughters, Polly and Susannah. Later, Susannah sold much of the property, stipulating that a certain portion of the land that held the family burial ground be left alone. But a later owner of the house knocked down the gravestones, losing the graves over time. Speculation claims to say that this could be a reason for the hauntings.

A macabre side note to this, Ron Ferland, who once owned Little Professor Book Center in Chesterfield Meadows Shopping Center until July 2006, said that someone once came into the bookstore and told him that the grave stones were still there among the hedges and not removed when the shopping center was built. Obviously, this is not true, but it makes for another interesting myth about Wrexham Hall. Ron said he has never believed this story and never searched for the graves.

When Stanley Hague owned the house, the Lady in Red was sighted. He had been working in the field across from Wrexham Hall when he and some workers noticed a strange woman dressed in red sitting on the front porch. All of them clearly saw her and commented on the red dress. But when he returned home later after the day's work, he asked his wife about her mother, and why she had been sitting on the porch dressed all in red. His wife answered with surprise that her mother had been in Richmond all day.

The ghost's presence continues to be felt there on a regular basis, and even occasionally seen. Other owners, Judge Ernest P. Gates and his wife, GeeGee, lived in the Hall for several years and had many encounters with her. GeeGee said that most of the time, it sounded like someone walking up the steps, and guests reported that they heard a rocking chair rock at night and could feel a presence in the house. Though GeeGee claimed not to be afraid, still she kept two television sets going so she wouldn't hear the noises. Years later, the later owners of the wedding reception business did the same thing, turning up the TV whenever they heard voices coming from upstairs, knowing that they were the only ones in the house at the time. The current owner does this, too.

Not long after the Gates moved into the house, their daughter, Gini, would hear voices in the hallway near the steps, just outside her bedroom.

One time when she had been decorating her room, she heard a woman say, "Oh, I like what she's doing—it's beautiful. I like everything she's done." Gini left her bedroom to check it out, but found no one at all. She checked the entire house, finding that she was alone.

Once, a family friend paid the Gates a visit. When they told her of the ghost, she scoffed and said it was utter nonsense. They sat in the main sitting room where the Gates had a full bookcase that went from floor to ceiling. One of the books flew off its shelf and nearly struck the woman.

Their son, Tom Gates, invited a teenage friend who played for the football team of L. C. Bird High School to stay the night. The rest of the Gates were gone, and they would have the place to themselves. The friend agreed and came over. Tom and his friend watched television on the upstairs passage between the bedroom and the door that led to the other section of the house. Suddenly, they heard footsteps; one door opened and closed, then the sound of footsteps, and finally, the other door opening and closing. Both ran downstairs and grabbed a shotgun and stayed up all night.

Other occurrences included family articles disappearing and reappearing, doors opening and shutting for no reason, and the occasional cold gust of air blowing through the rooms all of a sudden.

An interview with Ron Ferland revealed that he and his wife, MaryAnn, had an experience in the house just after it had been moved to its current location. About twenty years ago, they decided to check out Wrexham. They entered and discovered they could go up the stairs on one side and down the stairs on the other side. When they reached the top of the stairs on the one side, they saw a room and entered it, finding it very cold. Ron said that's what made it strange—it was the only cold room in the whole house! Later, they ran into a former resident of the house, David Gates. When they mentioned the cold room, he said that it had been his sister, Gini's, room, and it had always been cold like that.

Ron also talked about someone else who experienced something at the house when it was being worked on. He assumed the man was the supervisor of the workers. The man told him that one day he thought he saw something out of the corner of his eye and when he looked up, he saw someone in red at the window. He gave the description of something that looked like fog dissipating.

Tamara Evans of the Chesterfield Historical Society told the story of some painters who were painting the house back in the '80s. The lady of the house had gone to the store, leaving them alone there. One of the painters was up on a ladder propped against the house when he saw a woman at the window near him. He called out to the man below, "Look up here. There's this woman here." He thought she was flirting with him, as she looked coyly at him and would back away, then come back. When Mrs. Gates came back, they asked her about the lady in the bedroom and she replied that there was no one in the house at the time. It freaked them out.

Tamara told of the time after the house was empty. She convinced her husband and kids to go and take a look at it—see if it'd be worth getting. The children were excited at going to see a really haunted house. Once inside, they found some of the ceiling on the floor. Tamara asked her husband how long it would take to fix up the place and he said ten years, so that nipped all thoughts of buying it. They decided to still wander through the house and went upstairs. In one of the bedrooms, one of her children asked, "Is this the room the ghost haunts?" Just then, the door slammed shut. They left the house quickly.

Currently, the house is owned by Donna Brennan, who not only lives there with her daughter and young grandson, but also uses it for business purposes. There she holds weddings, receptions, and parties. It'd truly be a lovely place to be married in.

Donna said that many of the brides have admitted to feeling a 'presence' as they got ready in the bride room, which was formerly Gini Gates' bedroom, and the hair would stand up on their arms.

The spirit has made herself known to Donna, and to many others, as well. One of these incidents happened on the day a shaman came by, a child with him. The child, a psychic, started to talk to the ghost and confirmed that it was Susannah Walthall, who for many years people assumed the ghost to be.

One fall, when neither the air conditioning nor the heat needed to be on, Donna had four weddings planned for a single weekend. Sunday afternoon, the bartender began to complain of how hot it felt, as if the heater was on. It stayed that way until the last of the guests had left, and then suddenly cooled off. Nothing was wrong with the heater and putting on the air conditioning didn't work, either.

One phenomenon that happens more frequently than anything else is the voices on the landing outside the bride's room. One night, as Donna slept in her bedroom and her daughter in hers downstairs, the voices started, and both came out of their rooms, finding nothing.

Many times when Donna is alone in the house, she put on the television downstairs, turning the volume up high when the voices from upstairs start. She admitted to never going upstairs to check it out, something she said the former owners of the house and business said they never did when they were alone, either.

One Halloween, Q94, a local radio station, and the people from the Center for Paranormal Research and Investigations, stayed the night. CPRI used equipment to see if the ghost was real or not and actually recorded a female voice wailing. Something else very strange happened to one of the radio people. He came in at five am that morning to set up. The man was petrified to be there. The morning was still dark, but he had to have a smoke and so he went outside. As the morning lightened, he noticed on a chair in the front row, a veil lying on it that hadn't been there earlier. Even weirder, it felt dry and warm—impossible, as the chairs were still damp from the morning dew. He thought Donna played a trick on him, knowing that he had been frightened to come there. Donna told him that she didn't place the veil there, and no one else had either.

Another local radio station, 103.7, spent a Halloween there. They had arrived early to set up to broadcast, but mysteriously couldn't get a signal. They managed to get two of their listeners, Moe and Sally, to volunteer to stay the night in the bride's room. The next morning, Moe got up at four-thirty to five am to get to work and went outside to start up his car. Suddenly the car alarm went off, startling him. The strange thing about this was that he didn't *have* a car alarm. He, too, thought Donna was playing a trick on him, but she told him she hadn't, as she couldn't even program a VCR, much less anything electronic.

In order to make some meatballs, Donna once took off her diamond ring and put it on the window sill. She finished and left, then remembered she had left her ring, so she went back to discover that it had disappeared. She looked everywhere but didn't find it. Not until three weeks later did it turn up, on the kitchen counter.

Something else that disappeared, like the ring, and then reappeared, was a Time Life tape of some 1970s music by Barry Manilow. A couple who were to be married there brought it along with some other tapes to be used. Only that one tape vanished. Donna tried to replace the missing tape and ordered it from Time Life, but because it was a holiday weekend, Time Life said they couldn't promise to get it to her in time for the wedding.

And yet, the day before the wedding, the tape reappeared on a table in the reception room. Donna laughed and said that maybe Susannah didn't like Barry Manilow.

Donna said that Susannah apparently approves of the weddings happening there, maybe because she never got to have her own, since her fiancé died in the Civil War. At the wedding of a judge and a nurse who worked for Chesterfield County, the judge's brother took their picture. After it had been developed, they found someone else in the picture that hadn't been there when it was taken. With the couple, stood a red dress with a ball of light where the head normally would be.

I had a couple of experiences at Wrexham when I attended a meeting given by the Center for Paranormal Research and Investigations in the winter of 2006. The first one, everyone in the room where the weddings and receptions are held, saw. In one corner of the room, the lights were kept off to save electricity. At one point, a light came on, as if someone had flipped the light switch. The second phenomenon came later. Three other women and me were told to go upstairs and visit the "Bride's Room." After some time, two of the other three women entered the bathroom nearby. The third woman went back into the room to the other side and looked out of the window there. I remained on the landing. Suddenly, the door began to close, halting midway, as I stared at it. For the past couple hours, during the meeting, I had felt some kind of oppression, but the minute *that* happened, the oppression lifted.

Next time you're looking for the right place to get married or want to hold your wedding reception, or even just to have a party, try Wrexham Hall. You can find out more at http://www.theWrexham.com.

And maybe, just maybe, an uninvited guest of the insubstantial kind might show up.

Heading into the Haunted Bride's Room.

Chesterfield County Hauntings

Chesterfield County was founded on May 25, 1749, by the House of Burgesses. It was carved from Henrico County to eliminate lengthy travel by residents from the southern area to the Courthouse for business and court proceedings. The historic James River borders the county on the northeast and the Appomattox River forms the county's southern boundary. It received its name from the Fourth Earl of Stanhope, England's famed Lord Chesterfield. First settled in 1611 at the Citie of Henricus, the residents of Jamestown moved upstream to a "convenient, strong, healthie and sweete seate" after the conditions at Jamestown proved too harsh. The county's rich history included many historic "firsts," such as the Citie of Henricus established as second permanent English settlement in 1611. Tobacco cultivated at Bermuda Hundred a year later, and two years after that, Bermuda Hundred was the first incorporated town in America. Falling Creek had the first iron furnace in the New World. Mount Malady near Dutch Gap was the site of the first American hospital. Midlothian produced the first commercially-mined coal in America. Both the Midlothian Turnpike and the Midlothian to Manchester Railroad were the first paved road and the first railroad in Virginia.

With so much history behind it, it's no wonder there are hauntings.

Physic Hill

Physic Hill is a historic plantation in the Winterpock area of Chesterfield County. It had been named for the succession of doctors who inhabited it over the years. Built in two stages, it dates back to the early nineteenth century. The earlier section is a hall-parlor plan structure set on a high raised basement of three-course American Bond. A large side-passage wing had been added to the north slightly later—most likely in 1824. The house was badly dilapidated by the early 1970s, and exterior alterations, including the rebuilding of the west chimney and the removal of the east chimney on the hall-parlor section, were done. A lot of the original detailing remained in the side passage structure, including the double leaf front doors with two-tier transoms, a federal mantle with sunburst pattern, and an open string winder stair housing two original closets and decorated with sawn tread brackets, a curving wall string and a ramped, molded banister.

In 1983, the basement was a brick-walled root cellar. Local legend claimed that Dr. Walke used it to lock up and discipline slaves from Walke's Quarter. Slaves were also brought there to be examined by him before he had them sold off at a public auction at Physic Hill. The auction block used in the front yard was removed in the 1960s, and was put on exhibit at the Chesterfield County grounds.

In 1983, a couple, Ellis and Pattie Grady, moved into the place, knowing nothing of its history. They also knew nothing about the ghostly presence, though not long afterwards they began to have encounters with it.

Beginning on the upper floor, light would dim for no reason, and then come back up later. The pictures upstairs started falling off the walls. They would be replaced, only again to be found on the floor.

Physic Hill.

Footsteps resounded above the ceiling of the master bedroom close on the heels of the pictures falling. Pattie Grady thought that they sounded like human footsteps and were real and not imagined, as she tried to find a logical reason behind all the happenings.

Once, after the Gradys had decorated the house, they found the bed in an upstairs guest room taken apart, the mattress on the floor. It appeared that someone wasn't happy with what they had done with the embellishments. On Christmas Day, 1983, no hot water would flow from the upstairs bathroom sink faucet. Ellis Grady tried to determine the problem, but it was not the plumbing. The shower in the same bathroom had hot water when they tested it, and its water came through the same pipes that went to the sink. Also, on two occasions, the Gradys would find curtains down and on the floor. Nothing was broken or loose to cause the curtains to fall, and the storm window was up, preventing any wind from coming in—and yet, the curtains lay on the floor.

Pattie Grady dug into County archives, trying to see what she could find out about the place and its history. Besides information about the basics of the house, she learned that Dr. Walke was born about 1790, and married a Martha Branch, the daughter of Thomas Branch of Willow Hill. She passed away March 19, 1841, at fifty-two years and six months of age, and was buried in the family plot southeast of the house. Her headstone is the only marked one on the plantation. As for Dr. Walke, he died in 1863, leaving a personal estate appraised at $60,625 in Confederate currency that included forty slaves and a library worth $75 to be divided equally between his two sons, Sydenham and John Winston.

Pattie began to believe that the spirit was Martha. She couldn't find out much about her death, whether it was violent or not. She even thought that maybe Martha was angry with her husband, who'd married twice after her death and brought each bride to the house. The occurrences quieted down when they found a portrait of Dr. Walke in the house, took a picture of it, and hung the reproduction above the fireplace in the parlor. But the peace didn't keep the disturbances settled for long.

In September 1984, the Gradys decided to have the house painted. The family went out for the day and left two painters alone in the house. The next day, Pattie told one of the painters that he was painting near the ghost's window, and he began to look upset. It seemed that the day before, about dusk, as he worked on the end of the house near Martha's room, he saw a lady three different times at the window. Never saying a word, she watched him, and then dissipated. She had long brown hair that fell to her shoulders in ringlets and she wore a large piece of jewelry at her neck. Pattie thought he meant a necklace, but no, he said it was more like a brooch. He thought she looked to be maybe in her late forties or early fifties, was slender, and wore a dress with puffed sleeves.

Lauri Horner and Tamara Evans (Tamara is now Museum Shop Manager at Magnolia Grange) of the Chesterfield Historical Society came to call one time. Patti told Tamara that her maid would always become frightened when she was cleaning in one bedroom and would leave. Both women went up with Pattie to the bedroom. It had a fireplace, and they stood on each side of it, two feet away from it. The fireplace had a poker propped up inside and lodged in. Jokingly, Tamara asked Pattie, "Is this where the ghost is seen?" Just then, the poker made a sound like a *clunk* and fell at their feet.

Not long after, Pattie found a descendent of Martha's who lived in New York and had a portrait of Martha's daughter, painted in 1838. She had a photograph of it sent to her. Shockingly, Pattie saw a gaunt young woman, one who fit the description the painter had given her. In the painting, she wore a dress with puff sleeves exactly as he described.

It was Tamara Evans who said that the Gradys had moved out eventually, selling the house to the Hays. The Hays lived in the house for a few years and then sold it to a single woman who Tamara thought was a lady executive for Proctor and Gamble. She lived in the house for only a year. After that, it changed hands several times.

Online, at a realtor's website, there was mention of the house advertised for sale, but this was a year ago and the dwelling appears to be occupied again. Some of the history behind the house is on the website and there is also something about the haunting. The realtor said that the current owner reported that while she was sleeping with her daughters (her husband was out of town at the time), she woke in the middle of the night and thought she saw a shape at the foot of her bed. The shape was stroking one daughter's leg, very peacefully and lovingly. She drifted off back to sleep then, not knowing if it was real or not.

Magnolia Grange

At another historical house, Magnolia Grange, taken care of by the Chesterfield Historical Society and used for tours, there have been occurrences.

Built in 1822 by William Winfree, Magnolia Grange is an attractive federal-style plantation house. Named for the circle of magnolia trees that once upon a time dotted its front lawn, it is noted for distinctive architecture that includes elaborate ceiling medallions, along with carvings on mantels, doorways, and window frames. It is a Virginia Historic Landmark and is on the National Register of Historic Places. The families that had inhabited the house included the Winfrees, DuVals, and Cogbills—all whom made important contributions to life in Chesterfield County and the Commonwealth itself. The Grange hosts many special events. Even now, from October to December 2006, it is housing a funeral exhibit by J. T. Morris Funeral Home.

The home still houses spirits of those who lived there in the past. In 2005, a woman named Mary (Tamara thinks her last name was Downey) from Pennsylvania came by. A psychic, she'd been checking out places like Magnolia Grange for spirit activity. George Lutz, the man from the famous Amityville Horror haunting in the '70s, was with her. Tamara thought he seemed a quiet man and didn't say much of anything while there. Mary walked through the house and told Tamara of the lady in a 1820s Empire-style dress standing on the sixth step of the staircase, on the foyer. She said that the woman was friendly and petite in stature.

Magnolia Grange.

She went on to tell Tamara of the man in the parlor, tall, dark, and brooding. Her comments were that it was obvious he hadn't been born into money, but worked his way up, unlike the lady on the staircase. And as they stood on the landing, she pointed toward one room, asking if that was the children's room. "Yes, it is," said Tamara, and Mary confided that she could hear children's laughter coming from there.

Later, she went outside and said that she saw white-covered tables in the back yard, with ladies in long gowns having tea. (This same woman later went to Eppington, another plantation in Chesterfield, and claimed that she had felt something of a supernatural presence there.)

Another time, some members of the Red Hat Society (a club for women fifty and older) took a tour of the house, but refused to enter the Victorian room. They claimed that something, a presence, was in there.

The spirits of the past family are not the only ones to haunt Magnolia Grange. A member of the Historical Society did so, too—maybe as his way to say goodbye to his fellow workers. Last summer, 2005, as he had been working across Route 10, in the old Chesterfield County jail next to the original 1917 Courthouse, he passed away. Afterwards, lights would flicker on and off at Magnolia Grange, including in the basement where he had always worked on archeological digs.

A Chester Home

Tamara Evans went on to tell me of the haunting that happened in the home she grew up in, in Chester, when her now twenty-something son, Brandon, was young. He was taking a bath upstairs, soaping up his hair into spikes, and the bathroom mirror fogged up. When finally it cleared, he saw an old lady in a floral patterned dress looking at him from it. Frightened, he ran out of the bathroom and down the stairs in terror. He described the old lady and Tamara realized who it was. It was her Aunt Pokey who passed away in 1965, when she was ten years old. Pokey had died in the rocking chair she was found in, down in the basement. She had apparently fallen asleep and never awakened. Though she never appeared to anyone else, she decided to do so to young Brandon who had never ever seen her, making his description all the more truthful. To this day, Tamara said he never says anything about the incident.

Bellmont House

Another haunted home in Chesterfield is mentioned in Chester's Village News, a local weekly newspaper for Chester, Virginia. Appearing in an article dated, October 26, 2006, is the history and haunting of Bellmont House. It seemed that there has always been rumors of ghosts, mysterious deaths, and even a possible stint as a brothel in its past. It was built in the mid-1800s by John M. Snellings and inherited by Virginia Elliott Chiles Snellings on his death. In 1878, it was sold to the Old Dominion Iron and Nailworks

Company on Belle Isle. Superintendent Ned Archer lived in it until 1900. From then on, it was rented out until a member of the Chiles family bought it in 1911. During the Great Depression, William Sadler purchased it.

There have always been strange things going on within the home, first reported by Virginia Elliott Chiles Snellings not long after the family moved in. Locked doors wouldn't stay locked, and windows fastened tightly would open. Footsteps and whispers could also be heard.

The family conducted their own investigations into the peculiar happenings. The whole family would be downstairs in front of the fireplace and someone could be heard walking down the steps of the staircase. It was thought to be possibly the nurse, getting a drink for the children, but when they checked, both the nurse and the children were found asleep in bed. They locked the house up tight and barred any way of someone escaping. Not long after that, the sound resumed, accompanied by whispers. Searching the house revealed nothing.

One time, before turning in for the night, Virginia's father read from the Bible, and then placed it back on its stand. Suddenly, the oak bars holding the front and back doors closed, fell, and both doors flung open.

At one point, the paper said that the spectral presence had been nicknamed "George." But after the article was published in the paper, someone contacted them and said that the ghost was Melissa, who died at age twenty, around 1830-40.

The article went on, mentioning the other legends surrounding the house. One of those legends is about it being a brothel at the turn of the twentieth century. Another one tells of a man shot to death on the premises. When the house was being remodeled, William Sadler's son found two guns hidden over the door jamb, one being a ladies' pearl-handled pistol. One of the residents of the house dismissed the brothel and murder, thinking that the murder theory was started because of a teenage boy found in the nearby woods, shot to death.

Railey Hill

Midlothian, Virginia today is a burgeoning upscale Chesterfield County residential and commercial community. Situated approximately ten miles west of Richmond on U. S. Route 60 and the Norfolk-Southern Railway, there's a highway historical marker that states that Midlothian is probably the site of the first coal mines in the U. S. Scattered throughout the village are remnants of the Midlothian area mines—old homes, taverns, and buildings of colliery owners, along with a few dwellings connected with the French Huguenots, who are among the first European settlers in the Midlothian area. Structures that still stand on Old Buckingham Road are Trabue's Tavern, Melrose, Haley Cole's Free School, and the Smith-Vincent house. Fortunately, some natural landscape has survived and lines the roadside; day lilies, periwinkle, trumpet vines, and Queen Ann's Lace mingling in the shade of tall cedars, hollies, oaks, hickories, and other native trees. The ancient periwinkled oak grove standing sentry over coal miners' graves in Old Mt. Pisgah M. E. Church Cemetery is especially beautiful at the crest of Falling Creek Hill.

Also at the crest of Falling Creek Hill on Route 60 stands Railey Hill, a frame dwelling which once housed the superintendent of the Mid-Lothian Coal Mining Company. It was built around 1800, maybe even earlier, by Mr. Railey, the owner of Railey Coal Mines in Midlothian, designed after his home back in England. During the 1980s two different specters were seen there.

When Mildred and Carl Whitfield acquired it, Railey Hill was in bad shape and needed to be restored. The house had been empty for years and the surrounding neighbors called it the "haunted house." Inside, there are nine rooms and eight fireplaces. The original floors are made of Virginia heart pine. There are "witch doors," which means the doors have a cross on each one, as back in the nineteenth century it had been believed that this kept witches from crossing the threshold of the home.

Both specters were definitely male. One was a young boy. Mildred Whitfield, who witnessed the two ghosts, thought the ghost might be the twelve-year-old son of a superintendent of the coal mines who lived in the house in the 1800s. The boy died in a mining accident. Others claimed to have seen a boy ghost in Walton Park, so Mildred figured that the one she witnessed had to be one and the same. The other spirit she feels is a young Yankee officer who lived in the house in 1865. Words etched in the window pane in the parlor said, "Lt. Charles F. Branch, U. S. Army, address Orwell, Vermont 1865." Apparently, Branch loved the house, and using a diamond, carved the message on the glass. It is believed that it was he who led the first group of Union soldiers to the area during the time of Richmond's fall. With his troop of about hundred men, he had been sent on ahead of the siege to occupy and protect the coal mines.

Mildred Whitfield didn't believe in ghosts, and yet, she saw them. The first time happened in 1981, the other in 1984. She's not sure if the second time was due more to a dream than an actual sighting.

In her kitchen, just before midnight, she saw a wraith. A man's face floated across the breakfast room and she screamed for her husband to come. She took off after it, not afraid; but when she rounded the corner, it had vanished. She thought it might have gone down into the cellar, but the door was shut. Her husband laughed at her, but she swore she saw it.

The next time something happened to her was in 1984. As she lay in bed one night, a white form appeared at the foot of the bed. Small and chunky, it looked like a boy. She got up. It dissipated through the floor.

Today the house is empty, across the road from a shopping center and marked with no trespassing signs.

Coverhill

Another plantation home called Cloverhill has reported paranormal activity. Historically, it is famous for Lee's Retreat and includes the route across the Ettrick Cotton Factory Bridge along River Road in Chesterfield County that General Robert E. Lee took when he was cut off from the western route by Generals Pickett and Rosser. Lee was served lunch by Cloverhill Plantation owner Judge Cox, as recorded by the judge's daughter, Kate Cox Logan, in her book, *My Confederate Girlhood*.

Something else Kate mentioned in her book was the day her brother returned home from the Civil War. A bird was seen at the window. Back then, that was considered a bad omen. Strangely enough, he died the next day.

Haw Branch

Haw Branch Plantation is located thirty-five miles southwest of Richmond, in Amelia County. Its particular claim to fame is having more manifestations of psychic phenomena than any of the other haunted houses in Richmond, if not the entire state of Virginia.

Haw Branch derives its name from a small stream on the property; its banks are lined with hawthorn trees. The mansion is of Georgian-Federal architecture. For more than two centuries, Haw Branch has been a well-known landmark in Amelia County. Set in acres of green lawn, it is surrounded by magnolia and elm trees, and tulips, too. The house is built in a rectangular, brick-paved depression that resembles a dry moat. This not only serves as a gutter, but helps the rooms in the English basement to receive as much light and air as the upper stories. The house has a hipped roof and exterior-end chimneys flanked by three-bay wings, also with hipped roofs. There's a kitchen with a huge cooking fireplace and a fully equipped baking oven, along with an old weaving room filled with early plantation artifacts and Indian relics. Dependency buildings include a smoke house, school, and a two-family dwelling—reminders of the slave quarters that housed sixty-eight slaves in 1858.

The house has a tobacco leaf design in the interior wall woodwork and a hawthorn blossom in the carvings of some of the mantels. All of this is thought to have been installed back in 1815. The high-ceiling rooms contain eighteenth-century furniture, some that was originally with the house.

Colonel Thomas Tabb and his wife, Rebecca, were the first owners and settled in Amelia County before it separated from Prince George County in 1735. Tabb increased his holdings over the years from a trading post to become one of the largest landowners in Virginia. A Virginia State Landmarks Commission report says that he purchased the land that began the plantation back in 1743. From there, it grew, reaching 2,700 acres by 1798. Speculation is that sometime after the Revolutionary War, John Tabb, son of Thomas, enlarged the house and gave it its present exterior appearance.

The next prominent family to own the house was the Mason family, also active in state and national affairs. John Y. Mason, Jr., master of the house then, lost his life early in the Civil War. His widow gave the sheet metal roof to the Confederacy to be melted down into bullets. Close to the end of the war, when some of Hunter's Raiders galloped into the yard, she kept the bullets on the front porch while her daughter took the family silver, crawled out through a small door concealed in the attic paneling, and hid it in the eaves.

The Masons owned the plantation until 1872. The economic burden imposed by the Reconstruction pressured its sale to Colonel Murray Blacker of Great Britain. He bought it mainly to breed blooded cattle and jumping horses, and started an agricultural school for young Englishmen. He sold it in 1903, where upon it passed through many hands. At last, it stood unoccupied for years and sunk into ruin. It wasn't until 1965 that the place came back into the hands of the family of a past owner. William Cary McConnaughey and his wife, Mary Gibson Jefferson, bought not only the house, but the 120 acres that remained of the property. Mary also happened to be the granddaughter of the Mason daughter who hid the family silver from the Union soldiers in 1865. She remembered her grandmother bringing her out to visit; that it had been in dreadful condition, unoccupied, the windows broken out, and cows wandering through the English basement.

The McConnaugheys had to sand the floor eleven times, and since it hadn't been painted since 1929, it absorbed fresh paint like a sponge. Finally, with much of the home renovated, the McConnaugheys, their four children, and their two dogs moved in on August 13, 1965. It was three months later when the strange events began to happen. On November 23, 1965, in the early morning hours, they were awakened by a blood-curdling scream of a woman, seeming to have come from somewhere upstairs. Gibson and Cary ran upstairs and met their children at the foot of the staircase that leads from the second floor to the attic. The two dogs, Porkchop and Blackie, shook with terror. The next day they checked the attic, but found nothing.

Then exactly six months later, they heard the woman's screams again, loud, just before dawn. Again, they couldn't find the source of them. The screams occurred once again, six months later, on May 23, 1967. Six months from that date, on November 23, the family waited, armed with a recorder and flashlights, but nothing happened.

So they tried again, six months from that date. Though no screams were heard, they did hear heavy footsteps outside the house walking across the yard, and a screeching wail, too. They went outside to stand on the porch. Gibson recalled a definite sound of someone or something running. Next they heard a wail coming from behind the barn. The next morning the children claimed to have seen a giant bird in the moonlight. Though never seen again, its screeches could be heard several times, always on or around May 23 or November 23.

During an interview in 1984, Gibson said they could never find the significance behind those particular dates. The mysterious woman's screams stopped, but still, something always appeared to happen on those two dates. One night Gibson saw a cardinal flying at their fan light over the front door, which was strange in itself, because the bird should have been asleep by then, like most normal birds. The date? November 23.

The family had been in the house only a few months. They were watching television one evening when another strange occurrence happened. They all heard a loud thud outside that shook the house. As Gibson said, "It sounded as though a very heavy object, like a safe, had fallen from a great height and landed on the bricks of the moat." The family rushed outside with their flashlights, expecting to find something lying there. Instead, they found nothing out of the ordinary. This kept occurring over the years, both at night and during the day.

Ghostly forms have also been seen. Once, at one in the morning, in the summer of '67, Gibson had gone to the kitchen for a glass of milk before retiring. With the only light coming from the refrigerator, she spied a glimpse of something in the hall—a silhouette of a slim girl in a floor-length dress with a full skirt, not the wide fullness of a hoop skirt, but one from an earlier period. No features could be discerned. The girl was not transparent, but a white silhouette. For about ten seconds the girl stood there, and then she vanished.

Gibson's daughter had a similar experience a few days later and told her mother about it. She described a lady in white standing in front of the fireplace in the drawing room, then disappearing. Gibson McConnaughey learned later that earlier residents of Haw Branch had seen the same apparition. A relative told Gibson that her great grandmother, Harriet B. Mason, mentioned seeing a lady in white, and once was awakened from a deep sleep by a touch from the ghost.

A mention of one of Gibson McConnaughey's great grandmother's girlfriends caused other psychic phenomena to erupt. Lights blinked off and on when her name came up. Did the ghosts not like her, or was something else behind it all?

Strange, unexplained odors would also be noticed. Several times, the scents of fresh oranges could be smelled in the library, even though there were no fresh oranges in the house at the time and the frozen version was still unopened. An attar of roses wafted to Mrs. McConnaughey's nose when no flowers were in the house. And when she did research on the family history at the county clerk's office, she discovered some family unpleasantness involving her great-great-great grandmother and the husbands of her two daughters. Apparently, when the daughters married, their husbands signed a pre-marital agreement never to sell the property the girls had been given. But, by conniving, they gained control of the land holdings and were going to sell them. The triple great grandmother sued, lost in a lower court, won in an appeals court, and regained control of the property for her daughters. The next morning after Gibson McConnaughey conducted the research, she woke up to a strong aroma of fresh mint.

Other sounds besides the screams, screeches, footsteps, and thumps were heard at Haws. One of the McConnaughey sons and a friend camped one night in a surviving slave cabin. They heard the sound of a cowbell circling the building all night long. Of course, none of the cows on the plantation wore bells.

Other sounds occurred in the attic. At one time or another, what sounded like furniture being dragged across the floor, could be heard there, and when the family went up to check, the furniture remained unmoved. Neither could any birds or animals be found in the attic. Another sound heard in the attic was that of a rocking chair rocking, which was impossible as it was broken and no one could sit in it.

On one occasion, a humming could be heard in the basement, like an old English folk tune. Incidentally, there was a sealed room is in the basement that fascinated the family's cats.

The house used to be opened to the public, but since both McConnaugheys have retired, it no longer is available for view. They've had writers come to the plantation over the years looking for stories behind the hauntings. One young woman doing an article on haunted houses spent the night in one of the upstairs bedrooms. An admitted skeptic, she became a believer when sometime during the night she woke up to the sound of footsteps approaching her bed. The family's cat freaked out and bolted from the bedroom, but when she sat up, the sounds ceased. Turning on the light, she found nothing else in the room with her.

The most intriguing phenomenon involves the two portraits. The first portrait is of a young woman named Florence Wright. A distant relative by marriage to the current owners of the plantation, not much is known of her. Her parents owned a summer home in Massachusetts and she passed away in her early twenties before the painting had been completed. What was strange about the portrait is that the McConnaugheys were told it was done in color, but when they uncrated it, they discovered it as a charcoal rendering. Not one speck of color could be discovered, only black, dirty white and gray, with no signature of the artist to be discerned. The back of the frame left tightly sealed, it was hung over the library fireplace.

A few days later, Gibson McConnaughey rushed upstairs from the English basement of Haw Branch as she heard the sounds of women's voices in conversation. At that time, with the house opened to the public, she assumed it was only some people wanting to view the house, and nothing supernatural. But she found no one there and no car in the parking lot or the road leading away from the house. Over the year, though, five or six times, unexplained voices could be heard coming from the library.

One day, some months later, Cary McConnaughey was reading a newspaper in the library and happened to look up and saw that the rose in the portrait had started to develop a pinkish tinge, the girl's black hair was lightening and the grayish skin changing to the color of flesh. Slowly, over the year, the portrait shifted to pastel colors. Various people from art departments of nearby Virginia colleges had seen it since the time it arrived and acknowledged the metamorphosis to color. They also could not give a logical explanation for the phenomenon.

A psychic expert investigated and said that Florence Wright's spirit was tied to the portrait, due to her death before it had been completed—that she had the power to leach the color from it if she felt dissatisfied with where it was placed. But apparently, she liked Haw Branch; hence the reason the color was revived. The psychic said Florence had help from the spirits of two other women. Whatever the real reason, when the color returned to the portrait, both the changes and the voices stopped.

Another interesting fact about the picture is that when it was first brought there, the owner of it then claimed that a famous American had painted it, but couldn't remember the name. It was a year later that some of the answers came. During a summer evening in 1972, one of the McConnaughey daughters and her friend sat on the floor of the library, just beneath the portrait. They got up from the floor and went to the sofa, and just then, the portrait slowly slid down the wall until the frame's bottom crushed a row of porcelain antiques on the mantel shelf, then tipped forward, and went over the edge of the mantel to fall to the pine floorboards. The glass shattered all across the floor as the portrait landed face down on exactly the spot where the two girls had just been sitting.

The painting was undamaged, but the wooden frame was definitely broken. After the family lifted it up, they found underneath the backing of the frame, a brass plate with Florence's full name, her birth date, and date of death. Though they searched, they couldn't find the artist's signature anywhere. The frame was repaired the next day and the portrait replaced in it, with the glass replaced. The man who repaired it tried to find the artist's signature, but couldn't. When they arrived back home with the portrait, and took it from their station wagon, Gibson happened to tilt her end of the frame upward and just then the name J. Wells Champney appeared—signed in pencil on the apron of the dark mahogany table in the picture. It seemed that only under a certain angle of light could the name be brought into sight.

The second portrait is of a closer relative, Gibson's great-great grandmother, Marianna Elizabeth Tabb. Marianna was born at Haw Branch in 1796. She returned there in 1815 as bride to William Jones Barksdale. The portrait was painted around the time of her marriage and hung at Haw Branch for years. Later, the Barksdales moved to another Tabb plantation, Clay Hill, and spent their remaining years there. Marianna died in 1856, and in January 1861, Clay Hill burned to the ground. The portrait of Marianna was saved from the fire by cutting it from the molding used to frame it. After that, though, what happened to it was a mystery.

A century later, Gibson McConnaughey saw a copy of a book of pictures from an exhibit of paintings entitled, "Makers of Richmond 1737-1860," which had been held at the Valentine Museum in 1948. In it was the reproduction of Marianna's portrait listed as the portrait of Jane Craig Stanard, the woman who allegedly inspired Edgar Allan Poe in his famous poem, "To Helen." But Gibson knew it was Marianna, and not Jane Stanard, because of a copy of the original Warrell portrait in an exhibit at Longwood College in 1973. She wrote to the Valentine Museum and told them of their error in identification. The museum had learned that the Warrell portrait had been bought by a Richmond printer, J. H. Whitty, possibly in the 1900s. It was he who had identified the woman in the portrait as Jane Craig Stanard. He was an avid collector of all things related to Poe.

Once again, the trail grew cold, but later, the president of the Poe Foundation found Whitty's collection, bought by another Poe follower. The name of the man was William H. Koester of Baltimore, Maryland. At that time, though, another reproduction of Marianna's portrait was published in a biography of Poe and identified as Stanard again.

But the McConnaugheys, the Poe Foundation, and the Valentine Museum kept searching for the portrait. Koester passed away in 1964, and his painting was inherited by his wife and two sons. All but the Warrell portrait had been sold to the University of Texas. Gibson McConnaughey wrote to the Koester son, explaining the mistaken identity of the portrait and asking if they could borrow or buy it. The son's reply was that his mother wanted to keep it, but if they ever decided to sell it, the McConnaugheys would be contacted. Fate on their side, the McConnaugheys learned in June 1976, two years after the correspondence, that the portrait was to be auctioned off in Baltimore. Listed as the source inspiration to Poe for "To Helen," the auction owner was informed of the portrait's true identity. But though it was announced only as a rare old painting by Warrell, the brochure still described it as linked to Poe.

So Gibson stood up when it came up for sale, announced that it was her great-great grandmother and had absolutely nothing at all to do with Poe. She brandished her proof in hand. That negated the Poe collectors' bidding action, and the McConnaugheys were able to purchase it as merely an old painting. They took it home and hung it up in the drawing room at Haw Branch. The strange thing connected to this: most of the paranormal activity at the plantation ceased after the painting's recovery.

But that's not all to the story of the two portraits—there's a story that could almost be the result of fiction, particularly Edgar Allan Poe's fiction.

Edgar Allan Poe wrote the short story, "The Oval Portrait," about a man who stays the night in a strange chateau. He reads late into the night and sees a portrait of a young girl, set in an oval frame, hanging on the wall. He becomes absorbed by it. The man describes the portrait as having an immortal beauty, with life-like characteristics. He finds that the girl had fallen in love with an artist and married him, only to discover that her husband was already married to his career.

The artist wanted to do a portrait of his wife and she let him. For days upon days, he paints and became so absorbed in his work that he fails to notice that the girl is withering in health and spirit. But she continues to sit for him and just smile without complaint, as she dearly loves him. Almost at the completion of the portrait, the artist allows no one into the turret, and so deep into his ardor for his work is he that he never sees his wife's rapidly deteriorating health. Finally finished, he stands before it, entranced with it, calling out in a loud voice, "This is indeed life itself!" And when he turns to his wife, he finds that she is dead.

Haunted Prison

There's a prison in Powhatan, Virginia, the State Farm, around twenty-five miles west of Richmond. And yes, it's haunted.

It all started in 1995, in October, on Friday the 13th. A young man who had allegedly murdered his grandmother had been brought to the prison for processing. Whether this particular person was tied to what happened after, there's no clear proof, but a series of mysterious incidents began to occur.

The first thing to happen was that one Carl Tuten, a guard working the midnight shift at the time, went upstairs to run off some copies on the copy machine in the clerical department. The machine turned itself on. He checked it, but found no reason for it to have come to life. Suddenly, he felt another presence in the room with him—something evil that gave him an eerie feeling all over his body. Carl just had to get out of there, and as he left, walking past the treatment room, a strange laugh filled the air. He looked, but found nothing.

The next day he had to run some copies off again, and after shutting the door, felt the presence again, as if someone was there with him and watching him. He searched the room and found nothing.

If it had been just him, then people could say that possibly he was imagining things. But another officer admitted to feeling something wrong in the records department. On three nights, October 14th through the 16th, besides being extremely cold in the room, he felt like someone continued to watch him. The feeling left him when he exited the room, though it still left him shaken.

Another time, Carl asked another officer to open the door to the Treatment Room, as a doctor was coming in. The officer did. The door flung itself shut. No one was inside at the time and there was no wind to cause this. The officer admitted to having a bad feeling coming over him right then.

Another officer had an uncanny event happen to him when he was running off some copies. While waiting and reading some papers posted on the wall, something moved next to him, to his right. Looking out of the corner of his eye, he saw a man. However, when he turned his head to look, the man had vanished.

A secretary told Carl of the time a cold rush of air hit her, as if the roof had opened up. She wasn't the only one to feel the coldness either; others admitted to feeling it, too.

A sergeant, normally skeptical in nature, told Carl of seeing a face staring at him from one of the empty offices in the treatment area. Looking through the glass window in the door, he noticed a dark shadow moving across on the inside. Another officer said he had seen a shadow lurking inside the treatment area as well, and described it exactly as the sergeant had. At the time, he didn't know that the sergeant had seen, what appeared to be, this same shadow.

An inmate told of being wakened at two-thirty in the morning by a feminine voice. The voice had called out his name. Thinking that it was the nurse bringing him medication, he got up and went over to the front of the cell, to the bars. No one stood there, though.

When Carl Tuten asked if he had heard voices before, the inmate said that he had, but begged him not to tell, as he didn't want to be thought of as crazy and sent to the psychiatric ward. Tuten assured him he wouldn't and the inmate told him of the past week being "hell," that several times a voice would call out his name, and that it was always late at night and always a female voice. No one was there when he got up to check.

One night, a sergeant was in the records department getting some information. He heard water running and went to check, finding the water fountain on, but no one around. He turned it off, but then it turned itself back on.

Another officer worked in the main control area, operating the doors. The door to one of the gates had been out of order for several weeks. When its light came on, he went to check, looking down the hallway, but seeing no one. Puzzled, he wondered how it came on, especially since the door was out of operation. Several other door 'incidents' happened after that, like the time six doors in a control room opened by themselves—impossible, as they have to be opened either electronically or by key.

One officer witnessed a shower coming on by itself. The only way this could have occurred is by someone depressing a button; but, there was no one there. One night, another officer, along with Tuten, saw water running from a bathroom sink. They place a hand under the water—and didn't get wet. It was as though someone or something else was holding a hand under the water.

A couple of more strange things involved the inmates. During a thunder storm, fire balls came out of a cell, while another time a sergeant saw one inmate's eyes glowing orange in the dark. The sergeant also said he saw a weird glow all over the inmate's cell.

Other odd things happened, as well. Once, the computer printed out the words, "blood born" twenty-five times, and the numbers *666* kept coming up in different ways. When they processed one prisoner whose numbers added up to six, he was put in cell C-3 (the third letter plus three equaling six) and six copies of his form ran off. Many other things happened: doors opening and shutting for no apparent reason, toilets flushing of their own accord, an adding machine that kept turning itself on, disembodied voices, faces, and forms appearing and then disappearing. Another incident involved a potted plant that began to spin by itself in front of Tuten and two other sergeants. It spun from side to side, then stopped. Tuten said that if it started spinning again, it was a sign. The potted plant began spinning again.

Things could still be happening there, and whether it's due to that convicted murderer being processed on Friday the 13th, it's hard to say. But then, a prison holds a lot of bad feelings and more, and who can really say what can accumulate over the years in a place like that?

Scary Specters in Goochland

Goochland County is located between Richmond and Charlottesville, lying to the north of the James River and south of Interstate 64, in the fast developing, vibrant Mid-Atlantic corridor in central Virginia. As one of the most scenic locations in the Richmond area, Goochland is convenient to major East Coast transportation.

Formed from the original shire of Henrico in May 1728, it was named for the new Lieutenant Governor, William Gooch. In 1727, a petition had been made to the Royal Governor of Virginia by the House of Burgesses. The petition, presented at the colonial capitol of Williamsburg, created the county; the first county created after the original eight shires of the Virginia Colony. In 1728, Goochland stretched westward to the Blue Ridge Mountains along both sides of the James River, encompassing back then what today are the counties of Powhatan, Fluvanna, Cumberland, Albemarle, Chesterfield, Buckingham, Appomattox, Amherst, and Nelson.

Even more interesting is the supernatural phenomena that has happened there.

The Legend of the Waller Mine Murder

One is a folklore tale that could have come out of the writings of Edgar Allan Poe. In fact, with today's generation enjoying a ghostly story mixed with horror, murder, mystery, and more, this one could grace the modern silver screen quite well.

As with stories passed down generation to generation, the details have worn down and the names of the participants have disappeared. The last known version of this tale surfaced in a letter to the current editor of a Richmond newspaper in the 1930s.

The old Waller gold mine in Goochland County—forty miles up the James from Richmond—reopened sometime in the early 1930s, even though it had been shut down for about three quarters of a century. Mined actively in the 1830s and 1840s, it was considered the richest gold mine in the United States, with rich ore discovered there. Of course, this was years before the famous gold strike by Sutter on the American River near Coloma, California in 1848.

A large wooden house, about two stories high with gray, weather-beaten boards and gaping doors and windows, was not far from the mine. It was this place that was reputed to be haunted in the 1930s. Everything about it appeared to be empty of human life for a very long time. During the heyday of the mine, several employees of Waller Mine lived here.

Legend has it that strange noises could be heard coming from there, especially at night. Sounds like a despairing cry of someone about to pass into the unknown. These wails were apparently so frightening that no one would go near the place and people would hurry past it.

When the mine was open, not all of those who lived in the house were honest types. One of these dishonest men pocketed a sizable amount of the gold and kept it hidden in some secret spot near the house. Another man who shared the house with him followed him and discovered where he kept his horde. The legend says that a few nights later, occupants of the house awoke to a scream from the hoarder's room. When they rushed in, they found him unconscious on the floor, his head bashed in by a blunt instrument. He died, never regaining consciousness. His death was investigated, but nothing was detected as to who committed the crime or why, and the murder remained unsolved for years. When it finally ran out of the mother lode, the Waller mine was closed and boarded up. All the employees went off in different directions.

As sometimes happens in cases like this, the other man, who had followed the murdered man to his secret treasure, met with an accident himself years later and confessed to the crime. He admitted to sneaking into the victim's room that night to kill him. But when he stepped on a creaky board in the floor, the other boarder woke up and asked who was there. That's when the murderer swung down a pole ax upon the man's head with a heavy blow. As the victim screamed, he bolted back to his room and hid the pole ax, then joined the others seeking the source of the scream. Later, he buried the ax, and after things settled, dug up the gold and left for the North.

He never got to enjoy his ill-gotten gains, though. He claimed that the dead man haunted him day and night, and that he had suffered, never knowing peace, since he killed the man. But it seems that his confession didn't appease the victim, for strange noises could still be heard decades after the murder. As Goochland County old timers still remark, "He's still searching in vain for his lost treasure."

There are other hauntings in Goochland that include a disappearing corpse, a black dog, and a headless woman.

The Black Dog

> "And if a man shall meet the Black Dog once, it shall be for joy; and if twice, it shall be for sorrow; and the third time, he shall die."

"The Black Dog of Hanging Hills"

The black dog is a common occurrence in many hauntings, mainly in Great Britain. Stories such as this are surprisingly common and some of them notably ancient, enough to merit sightings of such creatures being in a class of their own in the ghost world. Ghostly black dogs have been seen throughout Britain with few counties being left unaffected, though the form and identity of the beast may differ. Apparitions of this sort may be distinguished from normal flesh and blood black dogs by features such as large or glowing eyes (sometimes only one), their ability to appear or disappear out of thin air or into and out of the ground; no head, two heads; or the ability to change their size or appearance.

The black dogs go under many names depending which county you are in. In the north of England, in counties such as Yorkshire and Lancashire, you will hear names such as Guytrash, Shriker, or Barguest; in East Anglia and Norfolk, you will hear Black Shuck, Skeff, or Moddey Dhoo; and in the south of England, you will hear names like Yeth or Wish Hounds. The origin of the word Guytrash is unknown, but Shuck can be traced back to the Old English Scucca, meaning Demon, while Barguest may come from the German 'Bargeist' meaning spirit of the (funeral) bier. The demon association is sometimes emphasized by the title Devil Dog. In the south, Yeth means *Heath,* while Wish, in a similar vein, is an old Sussex word for *marsh.* This name for the hounds is widely used in Sussex, but the origin also seems linked to the term "Witch Hounds," which is also common. Whether there is any connection between the two is unknown.

The names may only be referring to the fact that these dogs are often seen in wild country places. In many places, the dogs are seen as omens of death. To see one means either a portent of your own death or the death of a family member.

Goochland's Black Dog was said by the old timers to be as big as a young calf. It roamed the county, and sightings of it were reported near the State Farm, at the entrance to Thorncliff, and also at Chestnut Hill Bottom.

Often, like the traditional black dogs seen in Britain, it would appear out of nowhere, trot alongside someone on foot or horseback or in a buggy. Obviously, it hasn't been seen in modern times. Even though it looked fearsome and was very big, it didn't harm anyone. Some, though, didn't want the dog accompanying them and would shoot at the animal. The bullets would just pass through its body, frightening the shooters while the dog just kept trotting beside them.

A lawyer named P. A. L. Smith, Sr. used to walk from his home to the State Farm to catch a train into Richmond. Many evenings when he returned, the black dog would walk with him as he headed home.

A woman, who lived near the State Farm, claimed that the dog entered her house by opening the screen door. She said that it walked over to her old-fashioned icebox, unfastened the door, took out some food, and then shut the door, and left the house. An interesting side note about this woman's house was that other strange phenomena had happened there. Many would come to see the windows and doors of her house rock and rattle for no obvious cause, so when she told of the food-stealing Black Dog, many believed her.

The Disapearing Corpse

Another occurrence happened to a Dr. Morriss Barret. He lived at Mount Bernard, and no one can pin down *when* what he described happened. It was most likely in the later part of the nineteenth century or the early half of the twentieth century, because he used a horse and buggy. One night, he and his wife were traveling home after a visit to some friends.

Just as they reached Black Rock, halfway between Mount Bernard and Plynlimmon, Mrs. Barret spied a man lying in the road. Dr. Barret tried to stop the buggy, but not in time, and the wheels went over the person. He stepped down from the buggy and peered down at the man. Shocked, he realized that it was Jim Lewis, who had occasionally worked for him, but whom he hadn't seen for a long time."

As the doctor reached for him, Lewis vanished. It left Barrett dumbfounded. He knew it was Lewis, and yet, to watch him disappear like that unnerved him.

The next day, a man from the Richmond City Morgue called on Barret and asked him to come and view a body he had laid out in the morgue. He wanted Barret to identify it, and, because this was not uncommon to do, Barret went. When he returned home, he looked very upset. He told his wife that the body in the morgue had been Lewis's, and that Lewis had been dead for two weeks. Shocked, Barret wondered how he could have seen him lying in the road, while at the same time the man was dead in the morgue.

The Headless Woman

The last story's setting is the Plynlimmon House, a large frame house once owned by Judge Isaac Pleasants, who happened to be the cousin of James Pleasants, Governor of Virginia from 1822 to 1825.

The ghost that haunted the house had never been identified. According to the legend, it was a woman and she was headless! Dressed in a white gown that seemed tissue-thin, she would descend the stairs, a lighted lamp in her hand. Halfway down, she would fling the lamp into the air and then hurl her body the rest of the way down the stairs, screaming a terrible and blood-curdling scream. Before anyone's eyes, she would dissipate.

For years and years this went on at the house. Some people speculated that maybe she'd been an early resident and that maybe she'd tripped, fallen down the stairs, and died. There's no logical explanation for her being headless, though.

One night, someone entered the old vacant house, doubting the ghostly tales. They say that "seeing is believing," and when the ghost appeared, she did what she had done over and over before. After this experience, he told this story to others; and confirmed that he had also found fresh blood on the stairs where she vanished.

A Haunted House in Goochland

One more ghostly Goochland tale happened to me some years ago when I was with my husband and members of a *Star Trek* club, camping over at a member's parents' house that they had bought to fix up for their retirement. The house was reputed to be haunted by a female ghost who would come down the stairs from the second floor. This ghost had so frightened the caretaker that he would never go near the stairs.

Anyway, I, along with my husband and another friend, stayed in the house, as none of us had a tent or camping equipment. That night, I woke up to someone whispering in my ear. Frightened, and needing to use the outside potty, I made my husband get up with me to go outside. That night I lay awake, wondering if my whisperer would come back. She never did and I have never been back to that house, either. Now out of contact with that member, I always wonder if the ghost still haunts the house.

Pocahontas Parkway: Haunted Route 895

Route 895 in Virginia is the 8.8-mile tolled freeway between the junction of I-95 and VA-150 Chippenham Parkway in Chesterfield County, and I-295 in Henrico County. Route 895 is also named the Pocahontas Parkway, and it is functionally an extension of Chippenham Parkway across the James River to I-295. VA-150 and Route 895 are both freeways that carry mixed traffic with automobiles, trucks, and buses.

Construction of the Route 895 toll road began on October 13, 1998, and the original target completion date was April 2002. Part of it opened on May 22, 2002, and the highway was completed on September 20, 2002. It was built under a single $314 million design/build contract, and it was completed at a cost of $314 million, on budget. The projected average daily traffic (ADT) initially was 15,000 over the James River Bridge with 10% large trucks, and its ADT in November 2005 is just over 16,700. Its James River Bridge span was built with six through lanes and two auxiliary lanes. The highway has six through lanes from VA-150 to just east of the mainline toll plaza near Wilton Road (excepting a small portion on the west end of the bridge that is painted for four lanes now with the other two lanes reserved for the future), and four lanes from Wilton Road to I-295. Six-lane widening was completed on VA-150 Chippenham Parkway between I-95 and VA-76 Powhite Parkway in June 2002, so these two freeways form a seamless, modern freeway corridor. It is also the first construction project implemented under Virginia's Public-Private Transportation Act of 1995 (PPTA).

So what does this toll road have to do with ghosts? Well, when Pocahontas Parkway opened in May 2002, on the local news channels and in articles in the *Richmond Times Dispatch,* stories of three ghostly Indians were reported being seen by people, starting with a truck driver. This happened mainly late at night, around one am—Indians on horseback dashed along the Parkway, some even passing through cars and trucks. Drum beats and wild chanting came from the distant woodlands adjoining the Parkway. Spirits with torches could be seen from woody hilltops while others darted through and around the toll booths.

As reported in the article in the *Richmond Times Dispatch*, the Parkway had been built where Virginia's Native Americans once hunted, fished, and lived. Some folks even hinted at final resting places possibly being disturbed. And from reports of psychic investigators from various places on the Web, when they interviewed those who live in the area, many admitted to hearing the drum beats and other sounds for years. The thought that maybe building the Parkway was the cause of the sudden rash of hauntings didn't seem to be the answer after all. The ghosts just did what they had always done; there just was a six-lane highway going through the area now.

When the truck driver first saw the Indians, he thought that it was the local Native Americans tribe, carrying out a strange protest, perhaps angry that the new roadway had been paved over some long forgotten village. But the toll taker, to whom he said something about it, had heard and seen too many unexplainable phenomena since the road had opened, and knew they were ghosts, not living beings. At the end of her shift that day, she filed a report, and the *Richmond Times Dispatch* obtained a copy from Virginia Department of Transportation. State police were called in, but found nothing.

Troopers who worked the graveyard shift in that area claimed they responded to dozens of calls about the Indians. Two were even documented in the State Police incident reports.

The first was taken at 3:11 am on July 1, 2002. Two days later, at 1:44 am, the police returned to a call put in about a subject running back and forth around the loading dock. In both cases, the troopers found nothing.

Both times the specters were reported as having cloudy but fully-formed legs, arms and torsos, with only the vaguest outline of a head.

Both troopers and the workers at the toll booth have reported hearing Indian drums, along with mingled whoops and shouts, and the cries of seemingly dozens of voices that, on occasion, rose over the noise of passing tractor-trailers. Frenzied chants and yowls resounded long after midnight. There were those who say that maybe it came from a kennel of dogs nearby, or from geese and ducks. But as one trooper said in the *Times Dispatch* article: "I know what a bunch of hunting dogs sound like, and it doesn't sound anything like that."

There are reports of employees who work at the toll plaza seeing and hearing other things out of the ordinary, as well. One time, a female employee, walking through the underground tunnel that leads to the booths, saw out of the corner of her eye a black figure standing behind her. She just kept on walking and ignored it. A night or two later, her husband, who also works there, and the supervisor on duty, spotted a horse with an Indian standing beside it, on the side of the parkway. They watched it until it finally disappeared.

Many of these spirits seemed to have found simple pleasure in keeping the toll booth workers upset. They would do this by banging on the backs of the metal maintenance buildings. This became an almost daily ritual, heard by a multitude of workers as well as by scores of other reliable witnesses. Some say that an occasional happening still occurs, but on a less reliable basis. One night, a tollbooth worker enjoying her lunch break, suddenly lost interest in eating when her can of soda began to move all over the table.

Pocahontas Parkway: Haunted Route 895. Heading toward the Toll Booth.

An engineer for Blau-Velt, a subcontractor working nights to get the bridge completed, also reported seeing an Indian. He claimed that he and two or three other guys noticed a horse with an Indian sitting on it, right at the bottom of the bridge. They started toward them, because horses weren't allowed on the interstate. Both horse and rider dissipated. The incident was reported as a trespass. But as the engineer later learned of more reports of ghostly happenings in the area, he said, "It sent a shiver down my spine."

Deanna Beacham of the local Nansemond tribe said that what had been seen was certainly not a protest by Native Americans as many claimed. As she told the reporter in the newspaper, "We are anxiously awaiting our federal recognition." Such activity would bring more harm than good in getting the government to officially recognize Virginia's Indian tribes.

What people were seeing were real spirits of long ago Indians. After all, Deanna said, if Indians became the names of places, rivers, and streets, why not physical manifestations of that, too?

Chief Stephen Adkins of the Chickahominy tribe agreed with her assessment, saying in the newspaper article, "I have felt a tangible link to spirits past. All of the (Virginia) tribes without exception are of the Christian faith. But if you look back, there is a strong belief in the Great Spirit."

And there was evidence of Indians inhabiting the area 3500 B.C. to the 1600s. When William and Mary's Center for Archeological Research did a dig at the site in advance of the bridge's construction, they found plenty of Indian artifacts. Artifacts that scattered as far back as five or six thousands years, with a main village closer to Richmond. Edward Haile, an area historian who used modern technology to corroborate Captain John Smith's 1608 map of the James River, remarked that the site closest to Richmond was larger, and that the Pocahontas Parkway was also home to the Indians for a long time.

Ron Hadad, owner of Hadad's Lake picnic grounds, located less than a mile from the toll plaza, has been there for thirty-seven years. His mother lived in the house he lives in and she told him she used to hear a lot of hooting and hollering. Hadad had never seen any Indians himself, but he remembered his mother's face when she mentioned her experiences.

In 1992, Hadad's Lake hosted a state-organized re-enactment. Hadad struck up a conversation with a local Indian chief's daughter, who told him that there were lots of spirits in the area, and as he admitted, not of the alcoholic kind.

There have been investigations of the hauntings, both by the Center for Paranormal Research and Investigations, and by Paranormal Plus.

Nowadays there doesn't seem to be much reported on any ghostly happenings. Maybe the Indians have gone on to the Great Spirit in the sky, and maybe, just maybe, they're still there—just being quieter about it.

Look both ways when driving down the Pocahontas Parkway, for you never know what you just might just see.

Centre Hill
Mansion in Petersburg

To the south of Richmond is Centre Hill Mansion in Petersburg, a historical mansion that now serves as a museum. The Petersburg Battlefield Museums Corporation had obtained the lease to operate it as a Civil War Museum. In 1952, a private nonprofit group took charge of it as the Centre Hill Battlefield Museum until 1972. Then the Battlefield Museum Corporation handed the deed over to the City of Petersburg, with the understanding that it be used as a museum, as part of the original agreement with Edgar S. Bowling back in 1937. Restoration began in 1972, with work being done from 1974 to 1978, and finally, in 1978, it opened as a house museum. The house contains all the original Federal style, Greek Revival, and the later Colonial Revival style in its architecture and modifications.

What has all this to do with ghosts? Let's talk about its history.

Around the 1890s, after Buckner Townsend Bolling passed away, the Archibald Campbell Pryor family rented the mansion. That's when the ghost stories started. Sounds of Civil War soldiers would be heard entering the building, running upstairs, and then leaving through the front door—always on January 24th at seven-thirty pm.

Another ghost that is seen a lot is a woman at the window above the front entrance. When asked, Anne Brown, the Site coordinator, said, "No one knows who she is and no one has ever found out."

Beautiful inside, the mansion reflects the various eras in its history from the time the Bolling family owned it to when the Davis family inhabited it. Built in 1823 by Robert Bolling IV, the mansion began life primarily as a Federal Style house.

The Bollings arrived in America in 1660, when Robert Bolling came over from England. His first wife had been Jane Rolfe; grand-daughter of Pocahontas, and between them, they had one son, John Bolling II, producing what was known as the "Red Bollings." John Bolling remarried, and in 1861, his second wife, Anne Stith, produced the start of the "White Bollings." It was from this line that the Bollings who owned the mansion descended.

Robert Bolling IV's father, Robert Bolling III, and his second wife, Mary Marshall Tabb, had settled on a piece of land in the very heart of Petersburg. They had two frame houses built on East Hill, side by side, though intentionally many feet apart. Eventually, Centre Hill was built in the middle, hence the name, though the Bollings chose to call it "Bollingbrook." They had five children in total, starting with Robert IV.

Robert IV had four wives, starting with Mary Burton. The second wife was Catherine Stith, daughter of Bruckner Stith and descendent of John Stith, father of Robert Bolling I's second wife. The third was Sally Washington, who passed away one month after their marriage, and the last, Anna Dade Stith, who also happened to be the half sister of his second wife. He had five children in total. Robert IV joined the Virginia Militia at the age of nine during the Revolutionary War, was present at the surrender at Yorktown, served in the Virginia Legislature, and was on the Vestry of Bristol Parish, Blandford Church. He passed away on January 26, 1839, one month shy of his eightieth birthday. Centre Hill was passed on to his eldest son, Robert Buckner Bolling.

Centre Hill Mansion in Petersburg.

Robert Buckner had eleven children and served in the Virginia Legislature. He was a member of Vestry of Blandford Church and later, the Vestry of Christ Church, as well as being a member of the Free Masons who met at Blandford. Buckner built a mausoleum in 1855, and had the remains of every Stith line Bolling family member laid to rest into it. He also provided room not only for himself and Sarah, his first wife, but also for his eldest son. Two of Robert Buckner's three wives are buried there. According to the family genealogist, Alexander Bolling, he owned five hundred slaves at the start of the Civil War. It is believed he left the mansion well before the Siege began in 1864, living at a retreat home in Fauquier County near Upperville.

After the fall of Petersburg, Centre Hill became occupied by Union troops, led by General George L. Hartsuff. President Abraham Lincoln visited Centre Hill on April 3, 1865, to go over the local situation with General Hartsuff. This meeting took place only eleven days before Lincoln's assassination.

Buckner lived another sixteen years after the war ended, dying on June 28, 1881, at the home of his second son, Stewart, in Staunton, Virginia. He left Centre Hill to be managed by Townsend Bolling, his third son. The property was supposed to be sold and settled amongst the heirs, but in 1887, most of the heirs felt it wasn't proceeding quickly enough and brought suit against Townsend and another brother, John. The estate finally settled, everyone received their share, and Townsend got Centre Hill as his portion.

Townsend, who never married, lived at Centre Hill until his death in 1893. After his death, the family rented it out to the family of Archibald Campbell Pryor. Then Charles Hall Davis and his bride, Sallie Filed Bernard, rented it from 1900 to 1901. In 1901, they bought it from the Bollings.

Davis was a lawyer, bank president, president of the Chamber of Commerce, secretary of Virginia Consolidated Milling Company, and land speculator. His wife, Sallie, and he remodeled various rooms in the mansion. Around 1910, Charles Hall Davis began to have financial problems, with charges of him mishandling funds at the Virginia Consolidated Milling Company. Though found innocent of those charges, he also lost funds through a takeover of a firm he had invested in, and had to auction some of the furnishings at Centre Hill to recoup his losses. Not everything was sold. One of those items catalogued for sale was the pair of marble dogs that guard the front porch of the house.

More problems ensued, and by the 20s and 30s, he sold off most of the surrounding lots he subdivided, including the homes around the place. He hoped this would help, but it didn't, for in 1936, Centre Hill Mansion sold at public auction for $7,300 to Mr. W. J. Miller of Petersburg. Secretary-treasurer of Woremac, Inc., Miller wanted to demolish the house, but public sentiment stopped his hand, so he offered to sell the property at the price he purchased it for. Finally, Mr. Edgar S. Bowling of New York, , came forth and purchased it. He donated it to the Department of the Interior, National Park Service, to be used as a museum, making the donation in his wife, Mrs. Joe McIlwaine Bowling's, name.

With such a long history, its no wonder the museum is haunted. In 1991, Ann Brown convinced Bill Martin to start a Ghost Watch, holding it on January 24th, the night the ghostly Civil War soldiers trooped up the stairs. They did not charge participants, as they weren't even sure anyone would come; they didn't even require reservations. When the date arrived, they found 700 people waiting! After that first year, they began to take reservations right after the first of January, which always fill up fast, and charge $5.00 for adults and $3.00 for children, 7-12. Anyone can participate in this; just call the Petersburg Visitors Business Center at either (804) 733-2400 or 1-800-368-3595 after the first of January. But do it quick, and call early to reserve: they fill up fast.

An interesting fact about the steps the soldiers march up is that they are not even the original staircase from the Civil War era, but new ones put in by Charles Davis. And yet, like clockwork, the soldiers march up those steps at the same time each January 24th.

Photos taken in the house have shown interesting images. One photograph Ann has was taken during a Ghost Watch. It shows a woman, Evelyn, standing in the park across from the front entrance and three streams of light coming down behind her, with the school in the background ablaze with light. Funny thing about the school; no one was even there. Another photograph was taken in one of the rooms. Arms appear to reach out of the air for someone looking at something on the wall. Another photo had some orbs floating in it.

The spirits in the house are never shy. One time, a gentleman, Mr. Pryor, used for his bedchamber the small room which is used as an office nowadays. Ghostly hands would keep snatching off his blankets and tossing them to the floor whenever the lights were turned off. As Ghost Watch tour guide, Sydney Knapp, told one tour group during Ghost Watch, "Apparently the ghost felt the room belonged to him."

There are three pianos located on the second floor. One family who lived there often told stories of hearing one of them being played, but when they checked it out, they would find nothing but silence.

A reporter from the *Progress Index* came over one time to take some photos, but when he tried to take them on the second floor, his camera wouldn't work. When he stepped outside, the camera worked just fine.

The assistant for Laura Willoughby, the Curator of Collections, had an experience that taught her that ghosts are real. Always the one to make reservations for the Ghost Watch, she constantly poked fun about it, as she was a non-believer. A couple days earlier, before the interview with Anne Brown, she had been upstairs in the front parlor. When she turned around and looked across the hallway, she saw, not *all* of a ghost, but a skirt scurrying away. She told Ann she would never laugh about the ghosts again.

"One time," Ann said, "two ladies had come in looking for the museum's gift shop, and though that's in the basement, they went upstairs. Later they came down and found me, complaining about the lady who wouldn't let them in so they could go to the gift shop." She said, "I told them that there was no one upstairs." Both ladies had been shocked.

In 1995, a worker was upstairs on the second floor, restoring the fanlight for the upstairs window. Susannah went looking for him and Ann jokingly said that maybe the ghost had gotten him. Just then, he entered the room they were in. He said that he thought someone kept staring at his back, and when he had turned around to see who it was, found nothing. Ann said that maybe it was Bolling, checking up on him to make sure he did his job right.

One visitor to the house museum during Ghost Watch noticed some water droplets on the banister and tried to wipe it away, only to discover it was not water, but tear drops. She also mentioned that at other Ghost Watches, she had heard the ghost soldiers on the stairs and seen the face of the woman at the window, too.

Another woman from Colonial Heights admitted to feeling a presence on the stairwell when she attended a Ghost Watch.

In one article of the *Progress Index,* a lady, Sandi Bosha, and several of her friends, decided to take the Ghost Watch tour after feeling the presence of the lady at the window. One of the friends brought a standard compass. In several areas of the house, the needle moved. One of two places was near the crib in the bedroom on the second floor, the other in a back bedroom. Another friend, Jan Hartman, admitted she felt something in the room with the cradle, a woman with a child. It was her opinion the woman wouldn't leave, as she was searching for the child.

Over the years, people complained of having the feeling of someone watching them, doors would open inexplicably, and the woman would be seen again and again at the window above the entrance. The woman particularly has been mentioned in one book about ghosts, *Virginia Ghosts* by Marguerite DuPont Lee, now out of print. In it, Marguerite learned a lot from Mrs. Campbell Pryor, who happened to be Anne Banister, a direct descendent of the builder of Centre Hill. One of the incidents happened to Banister Pryor, Anne's child. One morning at breakfast, Banister had come in and asked: "Mother, where is the pretty lady who came and sat on my bed last night? She held my hand and talked to me." Banister described the lady, who fit the description of the lady at the window seen by so many. And she said that, even then, the ghostly soldiers marched up the porch steps at half past seven on January 24th. Friends would gather in the drawing room, waiting for the phenomenon. At the appointed time, the door into the office could be heard opening and the sound of tramping, as if an entire regiment marched. With the clanking of sabers, they would be heard going up the stairs and entering the room over the office. Twenty minutes later, they would be heard descending the steps, crossing the hall, and with a slam of the front door, apparently go out.

A tour guide, Evelyn Franklin, and a group that she took on tour at the mansion, had an experience with a lamp on a table on the third floor. The lamp began to sway back and forth, moving slowly at first, and then going faster, the crystal prisms clinking into each other.

When I read about the ghostly reflection of a woman in a mirror over a fireplace in the *Progress Index*, I too now remember seeing this peculiar occurrence in the mirror, thinking at the time that it seemed filmy on the left side. The phenomenon even showed up in a photo I'd taken—barely, but there to the one side of the mirror.

Ann Brown admitted to never having experienced any manifestation, when I pointed out that she had, in a way. She told about the other double windows in the research room downstairs, which have a large, heavy metal cabinet pressed up against them. There are times she find them partly opened and she would squeeze behind the cabinet to close them. Since no reason was ever discovered why this kept happening, she had no doubt something supernatural was behind the reoccurring phenomenon.

Ann admitted that her deceased father, used to say he saw spirits. Also a girlfriend of hers who babysat for her, told her that an aunt of hers, who passed away, had been there with Ann's mother in her home. But never had she experienced anything, not until the windows at Centre Hill.

But whether she believes in the ghosts or not, she said, "Every morning when I enter the mansion I say, 'Good morning' and every night when I lock up to leave, I say, 'Good night.' I have too much respect for the ghosts here not to."

Some Spirits of the Tri-Cities Area

Petersburg, Colonial Heights, and Hopewell comprise what is called Tri-Cities Region of Richmond. And though Centre Hill Mansion is part of it, it's not the only place to have ghostly manifestations.

One ghostly place is the Appomattox Manor in Hopewell. Built in the late 1700s, it had expansions added on later by the Eppes family. It was abandoned by the Eppeses during the Civil War, and General Ulysses Grant used it as his headquarters.

Stories of strange noises not of this world all start with a soldier. The legend says that a nurse hid a Union soldier in the wall of the basement when Confederate soldiers came to inspect the house. Unable to escape, he stayed there even after the nurse was taken away and he died. It is said that he can be heard scratching at the walls to be let out. But Jimmy Blankenship, the curator for the Petersburg National Battlefield, said he had never seen any proof for that story, that it seemed too much like something out of an Edgar Allan Poe tale.

He did report a ghostly sighting back in 1961. A caretaker for the manor saw one of the Eppes ladies in the east wing hallway, wearing old-fashioned clothing. It startled her, as she didn't think anyone was at home. She called out to the woman, who turned with a surprised look on her face and then promptly vanished.

Another house in Hopewell, Weston Manor, has two spirits haunting it.

One story is of a lady in a blue dress. She walks down the front staircase inside the house. Seen on numerous occasions, she's always crying into a white handkerchief.

Other stories include a ghost who filled bowls on bedside tables with water. This practice halted when a resident reversed the hinges on a door. Still another story comes from Gloria Lee of the Historic Hopewell Foundation. One weekend, she worked around the house, and when done, started to gather up her things. She noticed her keys were missing, so she called her sister to come and help her look for them. Both searched and found the keys under a table in the catering kitchen located in the cellar. The women didn't think they could have fallen under this table. Even if they were dropped there, Lee would have heard them hitting the bricks.

In Petersburg, there's Blandford Cemetery. A story connected to it is about a man who was buried there in a glass-topped coffin and his grave left unfilled. When his wife remarried, she replaced the glass top with a thick marble slab. Legend states that the slab would not stay in place. But Martha Atkinson, Site Coordinator for Blandford Church and Cemetery, said she has never seen it out of place.

Real-Life
Basis for a
Fictional Ghost Story

Though I no longer own the cell phone in question, nor have the N-Telos service provider, still, this happened in Chesterfield County a couple years ago and became the idea for "Call in the Night," my ghost story in *Beyond the Four Walls*, a chapbook of four fictional ghost stories published by Naked Snake Press.

It happened one night when the telephone rang in the bedroom. My husband, Bill, got up and ran to the computer office/sewing room, as at that time was where the only caller ID in the house was located. Hung up on the wall, under the cabinets by the computer, he turned on the light and peered at the number on the screen.

He came back to the bedroom, looking puzzled. "It has your cell phone number on the caller ID."

Full of disbelief, I blurted out, "What? It's on the coffee table in the living room."

He thought that maybe one of our two cats, Samhain or Ripley, had gotten onto the table and stepped on it, causing it to ring our home phone number. He went to the living room, but found both cats asleep on the couch, the cell phone turned off for the night and undisturbed on the coffee table.

The next morning we checked the caller ID again, thinking maybe he had imagined the cell's number on it, but no. To this day it remains a puzzle, wondering who, or what, used my cell phone to make a call to us. No one we knew passed away at the time, and no other reason could explain it. Whatever the case, it gave me the creeps and a great idea for a fictional ghost story.

If you'd like to read my scary story, "Call in the Night," plus the three other fictional ghost stories in the chapbook, you can order it by visiting the Naked Snake Press website, www.nakedsnakepress.com, or Shocklines at http://shocklines.stores.yahoo.net/befowabbypak.html.

Conclusion

I'm sorry, but we've come to the end of this supernatural tour of Richmond, Virginia. I hope it was an enjoyable one for you, and that you learned not only about the famous, or even infamous, spectral residents of Richmond, but even about our unique legends, too. Most of all, I hope you grew to know Richmond itself.

When you're in town, check out some of the places mentioned in the book. And maybe, just maybe, you just might catch a glimpse of a ghost, too.